Houghton
Mifflin
Harcourt

MATH
Expressions
Common Core

Dr. Karen C. Fuson

GRADE

4

Volume 1

This material is based upon work supported by the
National Science Foundation
under Grant Numbers
ESI-9816320, REC-9806020, and RED-935373.

Any opinions, findings, and conclusions, or recommendations expressed in this material
are those of the author and do not necessarily reflect the views of the National Science Foundation.

VOLUME 1 CONTENTS

UNIT 1 Place Value and Multidigit Addition and Subtraction

© Houghton Mifflin Harcourt Publishing Company

UNIT 2 Multiplication with Whole Numbers

UNIT 4 Equations and Word Problems

STUDENT RESOURCES

Dear Family,

Your child is learning math in an innovative program called *Math Expressions*. In Unit 1, your child will use place value drawings and charts to understand that the value of each place is 10 times greater than the value of the place to its right. This understanding is essential when comparing, rounding, or adding multidigit numbers. *Math Expressions* encourages children to think about "making new groups" to help them understand place values.

We call the method below "New Groups Above". The numbers that represent the new groups are written above the problem.

1. Add the ones:

5 + 7 = 12 ones
12 = 2 ones + 10 ones,
and 10 ones = 1 new ten.

$$\begin{array}{r} \overset{1}{}5,1\,7\,5 \\ +\ 3,9\,6\,7 \\ \hline 2 \end{array}$$

2. Add the tens:

1 + 7 + 6 = 14 tens
14 = 4 tens + 10 tens,
and 10 tens = 1 new hundred.

$$\begin{array}{r} \overset{1\ \ 1}{}5,1\,7\,5 \\ +\ 3,9\,6\,7 \\ \hline 4\,2 \end{array}$$

3. Add the hundreds:

1 + 1 + 9 = 11 hundreds
11 = 1 hundred + 10 hundreds,
and 10 hundreds = 1 new thousand.

$$\begin{array}{r} \overset{1\ \ 1\ \ 1}{}5,1\,7\,5 \\ +\ 3,9\,6\,7 \\ \hline 1\,4\,2 \end{array}$$

4. Add the thousands:

1 + 5 + 3 = 9 thousands

$$\begin{array}{r} \overset{1\ \ 1\ \ 1}{}5,1\,7\,5 \\ +\ 3,9\,6\,7 \\ \hline 9,1\,4\,2 \end{array}$$

We call the following method "New Groups Below." The steps are the same, but the new groups are written below the addends.

1.

$$\begin{array}{r} 5,1\,7\,5 \\ +\ 3,9\,6\,7 \\ \hline {}_1 2 \end{array}$$

2.

$$\begin{array}{r} 5,1\,7\,5 \\ +\ 3,9\,6\,7 \\ \hline {}_{1\ 1} 4\,2 \end{array}$$

3.

$$\begin{array}{r} 5,1\,7\,5 \\ +\ 3,9\,6\,7 \\ \hline {}_{1\ 1\ 1} 4\,2 \end{array}$$

4.

$$\begin{array}{r} 5,1\,7\,5 \\ +\ 3,9\,6\,7 \\ \hline {}_{1\ 1\ 1} 9,1\,4\,2 \end{array}$$

It is easier to see the totals for each column (12 and 14) and adding is easier because you add the two numbers you see and then add the 1.

It is important that your child maintains his or her home practice with basic multiplication and division.

Sincerely,
Your child's teacher

© Houghton Mifflin Harcourt Publishing Company

COMMON CORE

This unit includes the Common Core Standards for Mathematical Content for Number and Operations in Base Ten and Measurement and Data, 4.NBT.1, 4.NBT.2, 4.NBT.3, 4.NBT.4, 4.MD.2 and all Mathematical Practices.

Estimada familia,

Su niño está aprendiendo matemáticas mediante el programa *Math Expressions*. En la Unidad 1, se usarán dibujos y tablas de valor posicional para comprender que el valor de cada lugar es 10 veces mayor que el valor del lugar a su derecha. Comprender esto es esencial para comparar, redondear o sumar números de varios dígitos. *Math Expressions* enseña a pensar en "formar grupos nuevos" para comprender los valores posicionales.

Este método se llama "Grupos nuevos arriba". Los números que representan los grupos nuevos se escriben arriba del problema:

1. Suma las unidades:

5 + 7 = 12 unidades
12 = 2 unidades + 10 unidades,
y 10 unidades = 1 nueva decena.

$$\begin{array}{r} \overset{1}{5,1\ 7\ 5} \\ +\ 3,9\ 6\ 7 \\ \hline 2 \end{array}$$

2. Suma las decenas:

1 + 7 + 6 = 14 decenas
14 = 4 decenas + 10 decenas,
y 10 decenas = 1 nueva centena.

$$\begin{array}{r} \overset{1\ 1}{5,1\ 7\ 5} \\ +\ 3,9\ 6\ 7 \\ \hline 4\ 2 \end{array}$$

3. Suma las centenas:

1 + 1 + 9 = 11 centenas
11 = 1 centenas + 10 centenas,
y 10 centenas = 1 nuevo millar.

$$\begin{array}{r} \overset{1\ \ 1\ 1}{5,1\ 7\ 5} \\ +\ 3,9\ 6\ 7 \\ \hline 1\ 4\ 2 \end{array}$$

4. Suma los millares:

1 + 5 + 3 = 9 millares

$$\begin{array}{r} \overset{1\ \ 1\ 1}{5,1\ 7\ 5} \\ +\ 3,9\ 6\ 7 \\ \hline 9,1\ 4\ 2 \end{array}$$

Este método se llama "Grupos nuevos abajo". Los pasos son iguales, pero los nuevos grupos se escriben abajo de los sumandos:

Es más fácil ver los totales de cada columna (12 y 14) y es más fácil sumar porque sumas los dos números que ves, y luego sumas 1.

1.
$$\begin{array}{r} 5,1\ 7\ 5 \\ +\ 3,9\ 6\ 7 \\ \hline 2 \end{array}$$

2.
$$\begin{array}{r} 5,1\ 7\ 5 \\ +\ 3,9\ 6\ 7 \\ \hline 4\ 2 \end{array}$$

3.
$$\begin{array}{r} 5,1\ 7\ 5 \\ +\ 3,9\ 6\ 7 \\ \hline 1\ 4\ 2 \end{array}$$

4.
$$\begin{array}{r} 5,1\ 7\ 5 \\ +\ 3,9\ 6\ 7 \\ \hline 9,1\ 4\ 2 \end{array}$$

Es importante que su niño siga practicando las multiplicaciones y divisiones básicas en casa.

Atentamente,
El maestro de su niño

© Houghton Mifflin Harcourt Publishing Company

COMMON CORE

Esta unidad incluye los Common Core Standards for Mathematical Content for Number and Operations in Base Ten and Measurement and Data, 4.NBT.1, 4.NBT.2, 4.NBT.3, 4.NBT.4, 4.MD.2 and all Mathematical Practices.

► Model Hundreds

You can represent numbers by making **place value drawings** on a **dot array**.

1. What number does this drawing show? _____ Explain your thinking.

_____

_____

► Model Thousands

Discuss this place value drawing. Write the number of each.

2. ones: _____

3. quick tens: _____

4. hundred boxes: _____

5. thousand bars: _____

6. How many hundred boxes could we draw inside each thousand bar? Explain.

_____

_____

7. What number does this drawing show?

_____

VOCABULARY
place value

► Model Greater Numbers

Place value can also be shown without using a dot array.

8. What number does this drawing represent?
   Explain your thinking.

   _____

   _____

   _____

   _____

What would the drawing represent if it had:

9. 3 more hundred boxes? _____

10. 0 hundred boxes? _____

11. 2 fewer quick tens? _____

12. 2 more quick tens? _____

13. 0 quick tens? _____

14. 5 fewer ones? _____

15. 0 ones? _____

16. 4 more thousand bars? _____

17. On your MathBoard, make a place value drawing for a different number that has the digits 1, 2, 7, and 9.

18. Explain how your drawing is similar to and different from the drawing for 1,279.

    _____

    _____

Place Value to Thousands

► Practice with Place Value Drawings

Make a place value drawing for each number, using ones, quick tens, and hundred boxes.

19. 6   20. 3

21. 603   22. 300

23. 63   24. 32

25. 325   26. 285

27. 109   28. 573

Name _____   Date _____

▶ Practice Modeling Thousands

Make a place value drawing for each number, using ones, quick tens, hundred boxes, and thousand bars.

29. 2,596   **30.** 3,045

▶ Whole Number Secret Code Cards

1,000	100	10	1
1,0 0 0	**1 0 0**	**1 0**	**1**
2,000	200	20	2
2,0 0 0	**2 0 0**	**2 0**	**2**
3,000	300	30	3
3,0 0 0	**3 0 0**	**3 0**	**3**
4,000	400	40	4
4,0 0 0	**4 0 0**	**4 0**	**4**
5,000	500	50	5
5,0 0 0	**5 0 0**	**5 0**	**5**
6,000	600	60	6
6,0 0 0	**6 0 0**	**6 0**	**6**
7,000	700	70	7
7,0 0 0	**7 0 0**	**7 0**	**7**
8,000	800	80	8
8,0 0 0	**8 0 0**	**8 0**	**8**
9,000	900	90	9
9,0 0 0	**9 0 0**	**9 0**	**9**

► Whole Number Secret Code Cards

one	ten (teen) (one ten)	one hundred	one thousand
two	twenty (two tens)	two hundred	two thousand
three	thirty (three tens)	three hundred	three thousand
four	forty (four tens)	four hundred	four thousand
five	fifty (five tens)	five hundred	five thousand
six	sixty (six tens)	six hundred	six thousand
seven	seventy (seven tens)	seven hundred	seven thousand
eight	eighty (eight tens)	eight hundred	eight thousand
nine	ninety (nine tens)	nine hundred	nine thousand

► The Place Value Chart

Discuss the patterns you see in the Place Value Poster below.

× 10 (Greater) ←————————————

Thousands	Hundreds	Tens	ONES
1,000.	100.	10.	1.
$\frac{1,000}{1}$	$\frac{100}{1}$	$\frac{10}{1}$	$\frac{1}{1}$
$1,000.00	$100.00	$10.00	$1

Use your Whole Number Secret Code Cards to make numbers on the frame.

| Thousands | Hundreds | Tens | ONES |
| $1000 | $100 | $10 | $1 |

VOCABULARY
standard form
word form
expanded form

▶ Write Numbers Using Expanded Form

Standard form: 8,562

Word form: eight thousand, five hundred sixty-two

Expanded form: 8,000 + 500 + 60 + 2

Read and write each number in expanded form.

1. 73 _70+3_

2. 108 _100+8_

3. 5,621 _5000+600+2+1_

4. 4,350 _4000+300+50_

5. 8,083 _8,000+80+3_

6. 1,006 _1,000+6_

Read and write each number in standard form.

7. 40 + 3 _43_

8. 200 + 60 + 1 _261_

9. 900 + 5 _905_

10. 1,000 + 70 + 9 _1,079_

11. 5,000 + 30 _5,030_

12. 9,000 + 800 + 4 _9,804_

Read and write each number in word form.

13. 400 + 40 + 1 _441_

14. 1,000 + 50 _1,050_

Read and write each number in standard form.

15. thirty-five

   _35_

16. three hundred five

   _305_

17. six thousand, eight

   _6,008_

18. six thousand, one hundred eight

   _6,108_

Write the value of the underlined digit.

19. 7<u>5</u>6 _50_

20. <u>4</u>,851 _4000_

21. 6,<u>5</u>07 _500_

Place Value Patterns

► Summarize Rounding Rules

Use these rounding frames as a visual aid when rounding
to the nearest 10, 100, 1,000.

Nearest 10	Nearest 100	Nearest 1,000
100	1,000	10,000
90	900	9,000
80	800	8,000
70	700	7,000
60	600	6,000
50	500	5,000
40	400	4,000
30	300	3,000
20	200	2,000
10	100	1,000

Round to the nearest ten.

1. 87 _90_   2. 16 _20_   3. 171 _170_

4. 2,165 _3,170_   5. 5,114 _5,110_   6. 3,098 _3,100_

Round to the nearest hundred.

7. 734 _700_   8. 363 _400_   9. 178 _200_

10. 6,249 _6,200_   11. 8,251 _8,200_   12. 8,992 _9,000_

Round to the nearest thousand.

13. 1,275 _1,000_   14. 8,655 _9000_   15. 5,482 _5000_

16. 3,804 _4000_   17. 1,501 _2,000_   18. 9,702 _10,000_

VOCABULARY
greater than >
less than <

▶ Compare Numbers

Discuss the problem below.

Jim has 24 trading cards and Hattie has 42 trading cards.
Who has more trading cards? How do you know?

Draw a place value model for each problem.
Write > (greater than), < (less than), or = to make
each statement true.

19. 26 ◯ 29   20. 44 ◯ 34   21. 26 ◯ 62

Compare using >, <, or =.

22. 74 ◯ 77   23. 85 ◯ 58   24. 126 ◯ 162

25. 253 ◯ 235   26. 620 ◯ 602   27. 825 ◯ 528

28. 478 ◯ 488   29. 3,294 ◯ 3,924   30. 8,925 ◯ 9,825

31. 6,706 ◯ 6,760   32. 4,106 ◯ 4,016   33. 1,997 ◯ 1,799

34. 9,172 ◯ 9,712   35. 5,296 ◯ 5,269   36. 7,684 ◯ 7,684

▶ Discuss and Summarize

Patterns to Millions

Hundred Millions	Ten Millions	Millions	Hundred Thousands	Ten Thousands	Thousands	Hundreds	Tens	Ones
100,000,000	10,000,000	1,000,000	100,000	10,000	1,000	100	10	1
millions			*thousands*			*[ones]*		

The Patterns to Millions chart shows that each digit in the number has a place value name. When we read a number, we do not say the place value name. We say the group name.

We say the word *million* after the digits in the millions group.

We say the word *thousand* after the digits in the thousands group.

We do not say the word *ones* after the digits in the ones group.

To read greater numbers, say each group of digits as if they were in the hundreds, tens, and ones places and then add the special name for that group.

▶ Read Numbers

Use your Whole Number Secret Code cards to make the groups of digits as shown below. Put them in the spaces on the Reading Millions Frame below to read them.

28,374   123,456   458,726   654,321   92,148   789,321

Reading Millions Frame

million	*thousand*	*[ones]*

► Read and Write Expanded Form

Read and write each number in expanded form.

1. 32,568 _30,000 + 2000 + 500 + 60 + 8_

2. 820,149 _800,000 + 20,000 + 100 + 40 + 9_

3. 405,763 _400,000 + 5000 + 700 + 60 + 3_

4. 703,070 _700,000 + 3,000 + 70_

Read and write each number in standard form.

5. 20,000 + 4,000 + 800 + 10 + 7 _24,817_

6. 700,000 + 50,000 + 3,000 + 200 + 90 + 6 _753,296_

7. 300,000 + 3,000 + 10 + 9 _303,019_

8. 800,000 + 40,000 + 400 + 80 _840,480_

Read and write each number in word form.

9. 90,000 + 7,000 + 300 + 20 + 4 _97,324_

10. 600,000 + 30,000 + 4,000 + 700 + 30 _634,730_

11. 200,000 + 3,000 + 80 + 6 _203,086_

12. 500,000 + 20,000 + 400 + 1 _520,401_

Read and write each number in standard form.

13. seventy-eight thousand, one hundred five _78,105_

14. one million _1000,000_

15. five hundred sixty-three thousand, fifty-two _563,052_

Numbers to One Million

Name _____ **Date** _____

► Compare Greater Numbers

Discuss the problem below.

A stadium hosted both a concert and a sporting event. The concert had 101,835 people in attendance. The sporting event had 101,538 people in attendance. Which event had more people in attendance? How do you know?

Compare. Write >, <, or = to make each statement true.

1. 12,563 ⬭> 11,987

2. 14,615 ⬭< 15,651

3. 23,487 ⬭< 28,734

4. 83,342 ⬭> 80,423

5. 79,131 ⬭> 79,113

6. 126,348 ⬭< 162,634

7. 705,126 ⬭= 705,126

8. 532,834 ⬭< 532,843

9. 647,313 ⬭> 647,310

10. 198,593 ⬭> 98,593

11. 75,621 ⬭< 705,126

12. 1,000,000 ⬭> 100,000

► Greatest Place Value

Round to the nearest ten thousand.

13. 25,987 _30,000_

14. 13,738 _10,000_

15. 48,333 _5,000_

16. 84,562 _80,000_

17. 92,132 _9,0000_

18. 99,141 _100,000_

Round to the nearest hundred thousand.

19. 531,987 _500,000_

20. 701,828 _700,000_

21. 670,019 _700,000_

22. 249,845 _200,000_

23. 390,101 _400,000_

24. 999,999 _1,000,000_

► Round to Any Place

Solve.

25. Write a number that changes to 310,000 when it is rounded. To what place was your number rounded?

   _____

26. Write a number that changes to 901,400 when it is rounded. To what place was your number rounded?

   _____

27. Write a number that changes to 800,000 when it is rounded. To what place was your number rounded?

   _____

28. Write a number that changes to 122,000 when it is rounded. To what place was your number rounded?

   _____

29. What is 395,101 rounded to the nearest:

   a. ten? _395100_

   b. hundred? _395,100_

   c. thousand? _395000_

   d. ten thousand? _400000_

   e. hundred thousand? _400000_

30. What is 958,069 rounded to the nearest:

   a. ten? _958,070_

   b. hundred? _958,100_

   c. thousand? _958,000_

   d. ten thousand? _____

   e. hundred thousand? _____

Compare and Round Greater Numbers

Name _____ **Date** _____

▶ Discuss Different Methods

Discuss how each addition method can be used to add
4-digit numbers.

5,879 + 6,754

1. New Groups Above Method

Step 1	Step 2	Step 3	Step 4
¹	¹ ¹	¹ ¹ ¹	¹ ¹ ¹
5,879	5,879	5,879	5,879
+ 6,754	+ 6,754	+ 6,754	+ 6,754
3	33	633	12,633

2. New Groups Below Method

Step 1	Step 2	Step 3	Step 4
5,879	5,879	5,879	5,879
+ 6,754	+ 6,754	+ 6,754	+ 6,754
3	33	633	12,633

3. Show Subtotals Method (Right-to-Left)

Step 1	Step 2	Step 3	Step 4	Step 5
5,879	5,879	5,879	5,879	5,879
+ 6,754	+ 6,754	+ 6,754	+ 6,754	+ 6,754
13	13	13	13	13
	120	120	120	120
		1,500	1,500	1,500
			11,000	+ 11,000
				12,633

▶ Practice

4.	908	5.	692	6.	5,362	7.	3,786
	+ 653		+ 543		+ 3,746		+ 6,335

► PATH to FLUENCY **Practice (continued)**

8. 2,782
    + 5,246
    ——————
    8,028

9. 6,293
    + 3,862

10. 3,729
    + 4,541

11. 8,196
    + 3,865

12. 7,862
    + 2,839

13. 2,764
    + 6,648

14. 4,825
    + 2,467

15. 5,364
    + 4,754

► **Addition and Money**

Think about how to solve this problem.

Carlos is saving money to buy a skateboard. He saved $27 one week and $14 the next week. How much did Carlos save altogether?

Solve each problem.

16. Robyn's grandmother gave her $38 for her birthday and her uncle gave her $25. How much did Robyn get altogether?

_____

17. A parent-teacher club sold baked goods to raise money for the school. They collected $268 on Friday and $479 on Saturday. How much did they collect altogether?

Make New Groups for Addition

Name _____ Date _____

► Analyze Different Methods

© Houghton Mifflin Harcourt Publishing Company

New Groups Above

Step 1
```
  273,608
+ 591,729
─────────
        7
```

Step 2
```
   1
  273,608
+ 591,729
─────────
       37
```

Step 3
```
    1 1
  273,608
+ 591,729
─────────
      337
```

Step 4
```
     1
  273,608
+ 591,729
─────────
    5,337
```

Step 5
```
  1 1 1
  273,608
+ 591,729
─────────
   65,337
```

Step 6
```
  1   1
  273,608
+ 591,729
─────────
  865,337
```

New Groups Below

Step 1
```
  273,608
+ 591,729
─────────
        7
```

Step 2
```
  273,608
+ 591,729
       1
─────────
       37
```

Step 3
```
  273,608
+ 591,729
     1 1
─────────
      337
```

Step 4
```
  273,608
+ 591,729
       1
─────────
    5,337
```

Step 5
```
  273,608
+ 591,729
   1 1 1
─────────
   65,337
```

Step 6
```
  273,608
+ 591,729
─────────
  865,337
```

Show Subtotals (Left-to-Right)

Step 1
```
  273,608
+ 591,729
─────────
  700,000
```

Step 2
```
  273,608
+ 591,729
  700,000
  160,000
─────────
```

Step 3
```
  273,608
+ 591,729
  700,000
  160,000
    4,000
─────────
```

Step 4
```
  273,608
+ 591,729
  700,000
  160,000
    4,000
    1,300
─────────
```

Step 5
```
  273,608
+ 591,729
  700,000
  160,000
    4,000
    1,300
       20
─────────
```

Step 6
```
  273,608
+ 591,729
  700,000
  160,000
    4,000
    1,300
       20
       17
─────────
```

Step 7
```
  273,608
+ 591,729
  700,000
  160,000
    4,000
    1,300
       20
       17
+ ───────
  865,337
```

VOCABULARY
digit

▶ Find the Mistake

When you add, it is important that you add **digits** in like places.

Look at the these addition exercises.

$43,629 + 5,807$ $1,468 + 327,509$ $470,952 + 4,306$

```
    43,629              1,468              470,952
  +  5,807           + 327,509           +  4,306
   ─────── 11          ───────── 11        ─────── 1 1
   101,699             474,309             901,552
```

1. Discuss the mistake that appears in all three exercises above.

▶ PATH to FLUENCY Practice Aligning Places

Copy each exercise, aligning places correctly. Then add.

2. $2,647 + 38$

3. $156 + 83,291$

4. $4,389 + 49,706$

5. $135,826 + 2,927$

6. $347,092 + 6,739$

7. $15,231 + 697,084$

8. Write an addition word problem that has an answer of $43,568.

_____

_____

_____

_____

► Use Estimation

You can use rounding to estimate a total. Then you can adjust your estimated total to find the exact total.

The best-selling fruits at Joy's Fruit Shack are peaches and bananas. During one month Joy sold 397 peaches and 412 bananas.

1. *About* how many peaches and bananas did she sell in all?

   _____

2. *Exactly* how many peaches and bananas did she sell?

   _____

Estimate. Then adjust your estimate to find the exact answer.

3. 89 + 28

   177

4. 153 + 98

   251

5. 1,297 + 802

   2099

6. 1,066 + 45,104

   46170

Solve.

Tomás has $100. He wants to buy a $38 camera. He also wants to buy a $49 CD player and 2 CDs that are on sale 2 for $8.

100
−38 *Show your work.*
62−49=13
−8
5

7. How can Tomás figure out whether he has enough money for all four items? Does he have enough?

   yes

   _____

► Use Estimation (continued)

Solve.

Show your work.

Students at Washington Middle School collected 1,598 cans during the first month of their aluminum drive. During the second month of the drive, they collected 2,006 cans.

$$\begin{array}{r} 8 \\ +6 \\ \hline \end{array}$$

$14 + 50 = 104$
$+500$
$1,000 + 604$
$+2,000 = 3,604$

8. About how many cans did the students collect in all?

3604 _____

9. Exactly how many cans did the students collect in all?

3,604 _____

► Look for "Easy" Combinations

You can sometimes find number combinations that make it possible to add numbers mentally.

10. Add 243, 274, 252, and 231 vertically. **1000**

11. Explain how you can use number combinations to help you add the numbers.

_____

_____

_____

► Share Solutions

Find the total. Add mentally if you can.

12.
$$\begin{array}{r} 8 \\ 4 \\ 6 \\ +2 \\ \hline 20 \end{array}$$

13.
$$\begin{array}{r} 46 \\ 21 \\ +64 \\ \hline 30 \end{array}$$
120   11
131

14.
$$\begin{array}{r} 35 \\ 29 \\ 75 \\ +61 \\ \hline 210 \end{array}$$
100 10
90   10

15.
$$\begin{array}{r} 348 \\ 516 \\ +492 \\ \hline 1,416 \end{array}$$

16.
$$\begin{array}{r} 147 \\ 182 \\ 108 \\ +165 \\ \hline 5 \end{array}$$
200
300
400

Estimation and Mental Math

Family Letter

Dear Family,

Your child is now learning about subtraction. A common subtraction mistake is subtracting in the wrong direction. Children may think that they always subtract the smaller digit from the larger digit, but this is not true. To help children avoid this mistake, the *Math Expressions* program encourages children to "fix" numbers first and then subtract.

$$\begin{array}{r} \cancel{1,634} \\ -\ \cancel{158} \\ \hline \cancel{1,524} \end{array}$$

When one or more digits in the top number are smaller than the corresponding digits in the bottom number, fix the numbers by "ungrouping." For example, 1,634 − 158 is shown below:

1. We cannot subtract 8 ones from 4 ones. We get more ones by ungrouping 1 ten to make 10 ones.

We now have 14 ones and only 2 tens.

$$\begin{array}{r} {}^{2\ 14}\\ 1,6\cancel{3}\cancel{4} \\ -\ 1\ 5\ 8 \\ \hline \end{array}$$

2. We cannot subtract 5 tens from 2 tens. We get more tens by ungrouping 1 hundred to make 10 tens.

We now have 12 tens and only 5 hundreds.

$$\begin{array}{r} {}^{12}\\ {}^{5\ \cancel{2}\ 14}\\ 1,\cancel{6}\cancel{3}\cancel{4} \\ -\ 1\ 5\ 8 \\ \hline \end{array}$$

3. Now we can subtract:
1 − 0 = 1 thousand
5 − 1 = 4 hundreds
12 − 5 = 7 tens
14 − 8 = 6 ones

$$\begin{array}{r} {}^{12}\\ {}^{5\ \cancel{2}\ 14}\\ 1,\cancel{6}\cancel{3}\cancel{4} \\ -\ 1\ 5\ 8 \\ \hline 1,4\ 7\ 6 \end{array}$$

In the method above, the numbers are ungrouped from right to left, but students can also ungroup from left to right. Children can choose whichever way works best for them.

Your child should also continue to practice multiplication and division skills at home.

If you have any questions or comments, please call or write me.

Sincerely,
Your child's teacher

COMMON CORE

This unit includes the Common Core Standards for Mathematical Content for Number and Operations in Base Ten and Measurement and Data 4.NBT.3, 4.NBT.4, 4.MD.2 and all Mathematical Practices.

Estimada familia:

Ahora su niño está aprendiendo a restar. Un error muy común al restar, es hacerlo en la dirección equivocada. Los niños pueden pensar que siempre se resta el dígito más pequeño del dígito más grande, pero no es verdad. Para ayudar a los niños a no cometer este error, el programa *Math Expressions* les propone "arreglar" los números primero y luego restar.

$$\begin{array}{r} 1,6\cancel{3}4 \\ -\ \cancel{1}58 \\ \hline 1,524 \end{array}$$

Cuando uno o más dígitos del número de arriba son más pequeños que los dígitos correspondientes del número de abajo, se arreglan los números "desagrupándolos". Por ejemplo, 1,634 − 158 se muestra abajo:

1. No podemos restar 8 unidades de 4 unidades. Obtenemos más unidades al desagrupar 1 decena para formar 10 unidades.

Ahora tenemos 14 unidades y solamente 2 decenas.

$$\begin{array}{r} {}^{2\ 14} \\ 1,6\,\cancel{3}\,\cancel{4} \\ -\ 1\,5\,8 \\ \hline \end{array}$$

2. No podemos restar 5 decenas de 2 decenas. Obtenemos más decenas al desagrupar 1 centena para formar 10 decenas.

Ahora tenemos 12 decenas y solamente 5 centenas.

$$\begin{array}{r} {}^{\ \ 12} \\ {}^{5\ \cancel{2}14} \\ 1,\cancel{6}\,\cancel{3}\,\cancel{4} \\ -\ 1\,5\,8 \\ \hline \end{array}$$

3. Ahora podemos restar:
1 − 0 = 1 millar
5 − 1 = 4 centenas
12 − 5 = 7 decenas
14 − 8 = 6 unidades

$$\begin{array}{r} {}^{\ \ 12} \\ {}^{5\ \cancel{2}14} \\ 1,\cancel{6}\,\cancel{3}\,\cancel{4} \\ -\ 1\,5\,8 \\ \hline 1,4\,7\,6 \end{array}$$

En el método de arriba se desagrupan los números de derecha a izquierda, pero también se pueden desagrupar de izquierda a derecha. Los niños pueden escoger la manera que les resulte más fácil.

Su niño también debe seguir practicando las destrezas de multiplicación y de división en casa.

Si tiene alguna pregunta, por favor comuníquese conmigo.

Atentamente,
El maestro de su niño

COMMON CORE Esta unidad incluye los Common Core Standards for Mathematical Content for Number and Operations in Base Ten and Measurement and Data 4.NBT.3, 4.NBT.4, 4.MD.2 and all Mathematical Practices.

▶ Discuss Ungrouping With Zeros

Look inside the magnifying glass and discuss each ungrouping step.

1. Ungroup step-by-step: *or*

$$
\begin{array}{r}
{}^{9}\;{}^{9} \\
{}^{7}\,{}^{10}\,{}^{10}\,{}^{10} \\
\cancel{8}\,\cancel{0}\,\cancel{0}\,\cancel{0} \\
-\;3{,}4\,9\,2 \\
\hline
4508
\end{array}
$$

2. Ungroup all at once:

$$
\begin{array}{r}
{}^{7}\,{}^{9}\,{}^{9}\,{}^{10} \\
\cancel{8}\,\cancel{0}\,\cancel{0}\,\cancel{0} \\
-\;3{,}4\,9\,2 \\
\hline
4{,}508
\end{array}
$$

▶ Decide When to Ungroup

3. Ungroup left-to-right: *or*

$$
\begin{array}{r}
{}^{15}\;{}^{11} \\
{}^{3}\,{}^{16}\,{}^{12}\,{}^{15} \\
\cancel{4}\,\cancel{6}\,\cancel{2}\,\cancel{5} \\
-\;2{,}9\,8\,7 \\
\hline
1{,}62
\end{array}
$$

4. Ungroup right-to-left:

$$
\begin{array}{r}
{}^{15}\;{}^{11} \\
{}^{3}\,{}^{16}\,{}^{12}\,{}^{15} \\
\cancel{4}\,\cancel{6}\,\cancel{2}\,\cancel{5} \\
-\;2{,}9\,8\,7 \\
\hline
1{,}628
\end{array}
$$

▶ Other Ungrouping Situations

5. When we have zeros and other digits on the top:

$$
\begin{array}{r}
{}^{1}\,{}^{16}\,{}^{9}\,{}^{13} \\
{}^{6}\,{}^{10} \\
\cancel{2}\,\cancel{7}\,\cancel{0}\,\cancel{3} \\
-\;1{,}9\,6\,6 \\
\hline
0{,}737
\end{array}
$$

6. When we have the same digit on the top and bottom:

$$
\begin{array}{r}
{}^{13}\;{}^{17} \\
{}^{4}\,{}^{14}\,{}^{7}\,{}^{13} \\
\cancel{5}\,\cancel{4}\,\cancel{8}\,\cancel{3} \\
-\;1{,}6\,8\,7 \\
\hline
3{,}996
\end{array}
$$

▶ PATH to FLUENCY Practice

Subtract. Show your new groups.

7.
$$
\begin{array}{r}
634 \\
-\;256 \\
\hline
378
\end{array}
$$

8.
$$
\begin{array}{r}
800 \\
-\;691 \\
\hline
109
\end{array}
$$

9.
$$
\begin{array}{r}
9{,}462 \\
-\;5{,}678 \\
\hline
3{,}784
\end{array}
$$

Subtract. Show your new groups.

10. 7,919
   − 3,846
   4,073

11. 8,502
   − 3,749

12. 4,221
   − 2,805

13. 7,000
   − 572
   6,428

14. 4,650
   − 2,793

15. 4,605
   − 1,711

16. 3,120
   −   38
   3,082

17. 6,082
   −   95

18. 2,107
   − 428

19. 1,852
   − 964
   888

20. 3,692
   − 2,704

21. 8,715
   − 6,742

22. 6,000
   − 4,351
   1,649

23. 7,400
   − 1,215

24. 3,583
   − 1,794

Solve.

25. Jake has 647 pennies in his penny collection album.
The album has space for 1,000 pennies. How many
more pennies can Jake place in his album?

353 pennies

26. A ship is making an 8,509-mile voyage. So far,
it has sailed 2,957 miles. How many miles of the
voyage remain?

_____

▶ Relate Addition to Subtraction

Addition and subtraction are **inverse operations.**
Break-apart drawings help to show inverse relationships.

1. Write a word problem that requires adding 1,310 and 2,057.

   _____

   _____

   _____

2. Write the **addends** and the sum in the break-apart drawing.

3. Complete the two addition problems represented by the break-apart drawing.

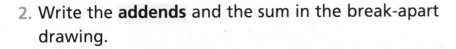

$$\begin{array}{r} 1{,}310 \\ +\underline{} \\ 3{,}367 \end{array} \qquad \begin{array}{r} 2{,}057 \\ +\underline{} \\ \underline{} \end{array}$$

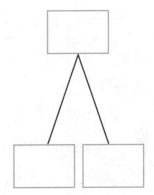

4. Write a word problem that requires subtracting 1,310 from 3,367.

   _____

   _____

   _____

5. Write two subtraction problems represented by the break-apart drawing.

Name _____   **Date** _____

► 〔PATH to FLUENCY〕 **Practice**

Subtract. Then use addition to check the subtraction.
Show your work.

6.   1,900
   − 574

Check: _____

7.   1,800
   − 1,216

Check: _____

8.   5,192
   − 341

Check: _____

9.   6,350
   − 2,460

Check: _____

10.   7,523
    − 3,424

Check: _____

11.   2,000 ·
    − 651

Check: _____

Solve.

12. In April, the zookeepers fed the penguins 4,620 fish.
    In May, they fed the penguins 5,068 fish. How many
    fish did they feed the penguins altogether?

_____

13. The head keeper knew how many fish the penguins
    had been fed altogether, and she knew they had been
    fed 4,620 fish in April. Write a subtraction problem to
    show how the keeper could determine the number of
    fish the penguins had been fed in May.

_____

Subtraction Undoes Addition

▶ Find and Correct Mistakes

Always check your work. Many mistakes can be easily fixed.

What is the mistake in each problem? How can you fix the mistake and find the correct answer?

1. 67,308 − 5,497

$$
\begin{array}{r}
12\\
6\;\;13\;\;10\\
6\,7\,3\,0\,8\\
-5{,}4\,9\,7\\
\hline
1\,2{,}3\,3\,8
\end{array}
$$

2. 134,865 − 5,294

$$
\begin{array}{r}
1\,3\,4{,}8\,6\,5\\
-5{,}2\,9\,4\\
\hline
1\,3\,1{,}6\,3\,1
\end{array}
$$

_____   _____

_____   _____

_____   _____

_____   _____

_____   _____

▶ Check Subtraction by "Adding Up"

"Add up" to find any places where there is a subtraction mistake. Discuss how each mistake might have been made and correct the subtraction if necessary.

3.
$$
\begin{array}{r}
163{,}406\\
-84{,}357\\
\hline
79{,}159
\end{array}
$$

4.
$$
\begin{array}{r}
526{,}741\\
-139{,}268\\
\hline
413{,}473
\end{array}
$$

5.
$$
\begin{array}{r}
1{,}000{,}000\\
-300{,}128\\
\hline
600{,}872
\end{array}
$$

6.
$$
\begin{array}{r}
5{,}472{,}639\\
-2{,}375{,}841\\
\hline
3{,}096{,}798
\end{array}
$$

7. Write and solve a subtraction problem with numbers in the hundred thousands.

_____

_____

► Estimate Differences

You can use estimation to decide if an answer is reasonable.

Dan did this subtraction: 8,196 − 5,980. His answer was 3,816. Discuss how using estimation can help you decide if his answer is correct.

Decide whether each answer is reasonable. Show your estimate.

8. 4,914 − 949 = 3,065

9. 52,022 − 29,571 = 22,451

_____

_____

Solve.

Show your work.

10. Bob has 3,226 marbles in his collection. Mia has 1,867 marbles. Bob says he has 2,359 more than Mia. Is Bob's answer reasonable? Show your estimate.

_____

11. Two towns have populations of 24,990 and 12,205. Gretchen says the difference is 12,785. Is Gretchen's answer reasonable? Show your estimate.

_____

12. Estimate to decide if the answer is reasonable. If it is not reasonable, describe the mistake and find the correct answer.

$$\begin{array}{r} 805,716 \\ -\ 290,905 \\ \hline 614,811 \end{array}$$

_____

_____

_____

Subtract Greater Numbers

▶ Discuss the Steps of the Problem

Sometimes you will need to work through more than one step to solve a problem. The steps can be shown in one or more equations.

1. In the morning, 19 students were working on a science project. In the afternoon, 3 students left and 7 more students came to work on the project. How many students were working on the project at the end of the day?

2. Solve the problem again by finishing Anita's and Chad's methods. Then discuss what is alike and what is different about each method.

Anita's Method	Chad's Method
Write an equation for each step.	**Write an equation for the whole problem.**
Find the total number of students who worked on the project.	Let $n=$ the number of students working on the project at the end of the day.
$19 + 7 =$	Students who left in the afternoon. Students who arrived in the afternoon.
Subtract the number of students who left in the afternoon.	$19 - \quad + \quad = \quad n$
$26 - 3 =$	$= n$

3. Solve. Discuss the steps you used.

A team is scheduled to play 12 games. Of those games, 7 will be played at home. The other games are away games. How many fewer away games than home games will be played?

▶ Share Solutions

Solve each problem.

Show your work.

4. The school library has 288 science books. Altogether the library has 618 science and animal books. How many fewer science books than animal books does the library have?

5. Olivia's stamp collection consists of 442 stamps. There are 131 butterfly stamps and 107 dolphin stamps in her collection. How many of Olivia's stamps are not of butterflies or dolphins?

▶ (PATH to FLUENCY) Practice Multidigit Addition and Subtraction

6.
$$
\begin{array}{r} 985 \\ -\ 792 \end{array}
$$

7.
$$
\begin{array}{r} 2,931 \\ +\ 8,563 \end{array}
$$

8.
$$
\begin{array}{r} 4,201 \\ +\ 9,979 \end{array}
$$

9.
$$
\begin{array}{r} 98,309 \\ -\ 48,659 \end{array}
$$

10.
$$
\begin{array}{r} 78,196 \\ -\ 14,587 \end{array}
$$

11.
$$
\begin{array}{r} 21,682 \\ +\ 95,436 \end{array}
$$

12.
$$
\begin{array}{r} 373,095 \\ +\ 185,543 \end{array}
$$

13.
$$
\begin{array}{r} 709,032 \\ -\ 239,125 \end{array}
$$

14.
$$
\begin{array}{r} 540,721 \\ +\ 375,699 \end{array}
$$

▶ Discuss Problem Types

Think of different types of problems for each exercise.
Write an equation for the problem then solve it.

1. $a + 278 = 747$

2. $b - 346 = 587$

3.

4.

_____   _____   _____   _____

_____   _____   _____   _____

▶ PATH to FLUENCY Share Solutions

Write an equation for the problem then solve it.   *Show your work.*
Make a math drawing if you need to.

5. Of 800,000 species of insects, about 560,000 undergo complete metamorphosis. How many species do not undergo complete metamorphosis?

_____

_____

6. The Great Pyramid of Giza has about 2,000,000 stone blocks. A replica has 1,900,000 fewer blocks. How many blocks are in the replica?

_____

_____

7. Last year 439,508 people visited Fun Town. This is 46,739 fewer visitors than this year. How many people visited Fun Town this year?

_____

_____

► PATH to FLUENCY **Share Solutions (continued)**

8. At the end of a baseball game, there were 35,602 people in the stadium. There were 37,614 people in the stadium at the beginning of the game. How many people left before the game ended?

_____

_____

9. This year Pinnacle Publishing printed 64,924 more books than Premier Publishing. If Pinnacle printed 231,069 books, how many books did Premier print?

_____

_____

10. Mary drove her car 2,483 miles during a road trip. Now she has 86,445 miles on her car. How many miles did her car have before her trip?

_____

_____

11. The Elbe River in Europe is 1,170 km long. The Yellow River in China is 5,465 km long. How long are the two rivers altogether?

_____

_____

12. A bridge is 1,595 feet long. Each cable holding up the bridge is 1,983 feet longer than the bridge itself. How long is each cable?

_____

_____

► Subtraction and Money

Sondra had $140 to spend on new clothes for school. She bought a shirt for $21. You can use a model to help you find out how much money she has left.

Sondra had _____ left.

Solve each problem. Use money if you need to.

Show your work.

13. Jason had $30. He gave $18 to his brother. How much money does Jason have left?

_____

14. Elana's coach had some money to spend on softball equipment. She spent $76 on bases. She has $174 left. How much did she have to start?

_____

15. The school science club raised $325. After buying equipment for an experiment they had $168 left. How much did they spend?

_____

16. Amy paid $575 for new furniture. Before buying it she had $813. How much did she have afterward?

_____

▶ Determine Reasonable Answers

Solve each problem. Check your answers using inverse operations.

17. Mrs. Washington has $265. She wants to buy shoes for $67 and dresses for $184. Does she have enough money? Explain your answer. _____

18. Terrell wants to run a total of 105 miles during the month. He ran a total of 87 miles during the first 3 weeks of the month. How much does he have to run on the 4th week to make his goal? _____

▶ What's the Error?

Dear Math Students,

My friend is taking a trip to Antarctica. He gave me $112 to buy him some clothes. I tried to buy a parka and two pairs of wool socks, but the clerk said I didn't have enough money. I added up the cost like this:

$98 + $12 = $110

Can you help me figure out what I did wrong?

Your friend,
Puzzled Penguin

Bill's Outdoor Wear

Pair of Wool socks	$12
Hat	$15
Mitten	$10
Parka	$98

19. Write a response to Puzzled Penguin.

_____

_____

Problem Solving With Greater Numbers

► Math and Bridges

Bridges are structures that are built to get over obstacles like water, a valley, or roads. Bridges can be made of concrete, steel, or even tree roots. Engineers and designers do a lot of math to be sure a bridge will stand up to its use and the forces of nature that affect it.

Lengths of Bridges		
Bridge	**Length Over Water (ft)**	
Manchac Swamp Bridge, U.S.A.	121,440	
Hangzhou Bay Bridge, China	117,057	
Lake Pontchartrain Causeway, U.S.A.	125,664	
Jiaozhou Bay Bridge, China	139,392	

1. Use the data in the table above to make a bar graph.

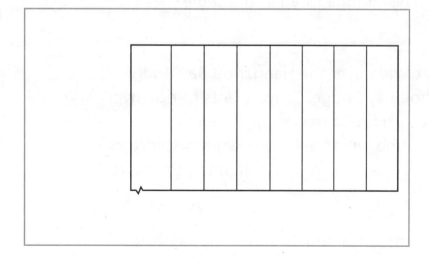

► Add and Subtract Greater Numbers

Lake Pontchartrain Causeway, U.S.A

For Exercises 2–5, use the data in the table on Student Book page 35.

use the data in the table on Student Book page 35.

Show your work.

2. How much longer is the Lake Pontchartrain Causeway than the Hangzhou Bay Bridge?

3. What is the difference in length between the longest bridge and shortest bridge listed in the table?

4. Liang's goal is to ride over the Hangzhou Bay Bridge and the Jiaozhou Bay Bridge. Tanya wants to ride over the Lake Pontchartrain Causeway and the Manchac Swamp Bridge. Who will travel the greater distance on the bridges? How many more feet will he or she travel?

5. The Danyang-Kunshan Grand Bridge in China is the longest bridge over land and water in the world. It is 401,308 feet longer than the Jiaozhou Bay Bridge. How long is the Danyan-Kunshan Grand Bridge?

Focus on Mathematical Practices

► Vocabulary

Choose the best term from the box.

1. Addition and subtraction are _____
because one operation undoes the other. **(Lesson 1-10)**

2. 3,957 and 4,218 are the _____ in the
problem 3,957 + 4,218. **(Lessons 1-11, 1-13)**

► Concepts and Skills

3. Use expanded form to explain how the value of the digit 4 in
the number 4,444 changes for each place value. **(Lesson 1-2)**

_____

_____

4. Which is greater, the value of the digit 6 in 650 or the
value of the digit 6 in 760? Explain. **(Lesson 1-2)**

_____

_____

5. Which of these numbers has the digit 7 with a value of
700: 7,352, 720, 270, 357? Explain. **(Lesson 1-2)**

_____

_____

Read and write the number in another form. (Lesson 1-4)

6. 453,208 in word form: _____

7. ninety thousand, thirty-three in standard form: _____

8. 680,742 in expanded form _____

Compare using >, <, or =. (Lesson 1-3, 1-5)

9. 84,055 ◯ 84,505   10. 7,862 ◯ 7,826   11. 369,125 ◯ 396,124

Round each number to the place value of the underlined digit.
(Lesson 1-3, 1-5)

12. 3<u>3</u>,875 _____

13. <u>9</u>20,812 _____

Add or subtract. (Lessons 1-6, 1-7, 1-9, 1-10, 1-11, 1-12)

14.   1,472
  + 5,178

15.   58,290
  − 31,602

16.   483,958
  + 126,081

17.   795,236
  − 478,517

▶ Problem Solving

Solve.

18. There were 3,982 people at the soccer game on Thursday. There were 1,886 more people at the soccer game on Saturday. How many people in all attended both games? (Lessons 1-6, 1-12)

_____

19. One machine makes 125,200 small paper clips in one day. Another machine makes 83,650 large paper clips in one day. How many fewer large paper clips than small paper clips are made in one day? (Lessons 1-11, 1-12, 1-13)

_____

20. **Extended Response** Determine whether the following statement is true or false. Explain your thinking. (Lessons 1-6, 1-9, 1-10)

6,421 − (284 + 653) = (6,421 − 284) + 653

_____

_____

Dear Family,

In this unit, your child will be learning about the common multiplication method that most adults know. However, they will also explore ways to draw multiplication. *Math Expressions* uses area of rectangles to show multiplication.

	30	+	7
20	20 × 30 = 600		20 × 7 = 140
+			
4	4 × 30 = 120		4 × 7 = 28

Area Method:

20 × 30 = 600
20 × 7 = 140
4 × 30 = 120
4 × 7 = 28
Total = 888

Shortcut Method:

$$\overset{1}{}\overset{2}{}$$
$$\begin{array}{r} 37 \\ \times\ 24 \\ \hline 148 \\ 74 \\ \hline 888 \end{array}$$

Area drawings help all students see multiplication. They also help students remember what numbers they need to multiply and what numbers make up the total.

Your child will also learn to find products involving single-digit numbers, tens, and hundreds by factoring the tens or hundreds. For example,

$$200 \times 30 = 2 \times 100 \times 3 \times 10$$
$$= 2 \times 3 \times 100 \times 10$$
$$= 6 \times 1{,}000 = 6{,}000$$

By observing the zeros patterns in products like these, your child will learn to do such multiplications mentally.

If your child is still not confident with single-digit multiplication and division, we urge you to set aside a few minutes every night for multiplication and division practice. In a few more weeks, the class will be doing multidigit division, so it is very important that your child be both fast and accurate with basic multiplication and division.

If you need practice materials, please contact me.

Sincerely,
Your child's teacher

COMMON CORE

This unit includes the Common Core Standards for Mathematical Content for Operations and Algebraic Thinking, Number and Operations in Base Ten and Measurement and Data, 4.OA.3, 4.NBT.1, 4.NBT.2, 4.NBT.3, 4.NBT.5, 4.MD.2 and all Mathematical Practices.

Estimada familia:

En esta unidad, su niño estará aprendiendo el método de multiplicación común que la mayoría de los adultos conoce. Sin embargo, también explorará maneras de dibujar la multiplicación. Para mostrar la multiplicación, *Math Expressions* usa el método del área del rectángulo.

	30	+	7
20	$20 \times 30 = 600$		$20 \times 7 = 140$
+			
4	$4 \times 30 = 120$		$4 \times 7 = 28$

Método del área

$20 \times 30 = 600$
$20 \times 7 = 140$
$4 \times 30 = 120$
$4 \times 7 = 28$
Total $= 888$

Método más corto

$$\begin{array}{r} {\scriptstyle 1} \\ {\scriptstyle 2} \\ 37 \\ \times\ 24 \\ \hline 148 \\ 74 \\ \hline 888 \end{array}$$

Los dibujos de área ayudan a los estudiantes a visualizar la multiplicación. También los ayuda a recordar cuáles números tienen que multiplicar y cuáles números forman el total.

Su niño también aprenderá a hallar productos relacionados con números de un solo dígito, con decenas y con centenas, factorizando las decenas o las centenas. Por ejemplo:

$$200 \times 30 = 2 \times 100 \times 3 \times 10$$
$$= 2 \times 3 \times 100 \times 10$$
$$= 6 \times 1,000 = 6,000$$

Al observar los patrones de ceros en productos como estos, su niño aprenderá a hacer dichas multiplicaciones mentalmente.

Si su niño todavía no domina la multiplicación y la división con números de un solo dígito, le sugerimos que dedique algunos minutos todas las noches para practicar la multiplicación y la división. Dentro de pocas semanas, la clase hará divisiones con números de varios dígitos, por eso es muy importante que su niño haga las operaciones básicas de multiplicación y de división de manera rápida y exacta.

Si necesita materiales para practicar, comuníquese conmigo.

Atentamente,
El maestro de su niño

Esta unidad incluye los Common Core Standards for Mathematical Content for Operations and Algebraic Thinking, Number and Operations in Base Ten and Measurement and Data, 4.OA.3, 4.NBT.1, 4.NBT.2, 4.NBT.3, 4.NBT.5, 4.MD.2 and all Mathematical Practices.

COMMON CORE

Arrays and Area Models

Class Activity

Name _____ Date _____

VOCABULARY
array
area

▶ Model a Product of Ones

> The number of unit squares in an **array** of connected unit squares is the
> **area** of the rectangle formed by the squares. We sometimes just show the
> measurement of length and width.
>
>
>
> You can draw a rectangle for any multiplication. In the real world, we use
> multiplication for finding both sizes of arrays and areas of figures.

A 2 × 3 rectangle has 6 unit squares inside, so 2 × 3 = 6.

1. On your MathBoard, draw a 3 × 2 rectangle. How is the
   3 × 2 rectangle similar to the 2 × 3 rectangle? How is it
   different?

   _____

   _____

   _____

   _____

2. How do the areas of the 2 × 3 and 3 × 2 rectangles
   compare?

   _____

   _____

© Houghton Mifflin Harcourt Publishing Company

UNIT 2 LESSON 1   Arrays and Area Models **41**

▶ Factor the Tens to Multiply Ones and Tens

This 2 × 30 rectangle contains 2 groups of 30 unit squares.

```
                    30
1 ┌─────────────────────────────────────┐ 1
+ │           1 × 30 = 30                │ +
1 │           1 × 30 = 30                │ 1
  └─────────────────────────────────────┘
                    30
```

This 2 × 30 rectangle contains 3 groups of 20 unit squares.

```
  30 =      10          +       10          +       10
  ┌───────────────┬───────────────┬───────────────┐
2 │  2 × 10 = 20  │  2 × 10 = 20  │  2 × 10 = 20  │ 2
  └───────────────┴───────────────┴───────────────┘
        10        +       10        +       10
```

This 2 × 30 rectangle contains 6 groups of 10 unit squares,
so its area is 60 **square units**.

```
  30 =     10          +      10          +      10
  ┌──────────────┬──────────────┬──────────────┐
1 │ 1 × 10 = 10  │ 1 × 10 = 10  │ 1 × 10 = 10  │ 1
1 │ 1 × 10 = 10  │ 1 × 10 = 10  │ 1 × 10 = 10  │ 1
  └──────────────┴──────────────┴──────────────┘
        10       +      10       +      10
```

3. How can we show this numerically? Complete the steps.

   $2 \times 30 = (2 \times 1) \times (\underline{\hspace{1cm}} \times 10)$

   $ = (\underline{\hspace{1cm}} \times \underline{\hspace{1cm}}) \times (1 \times 10)$

   $ = \underline{\hspace{1cm}} \times 10 = 60$

4. On your MathBoard, draw a 30 × 2 rectangle and
   find its area.

   _____

5. How is the 30 × 2 rectangle similar to the 2 × 30 rectangle?
   How is it different?

   _____

   _____

   _____

   _____

Arrays and Area Models

► Use Place Value to Multiply

You have learned about the Base Ten Pattern in place value. This model shows how place value and multiplication are connected.

You can use properties to show the relationship between place value and multiplication.

Associative Property $10 \times 20 = 10 \times (2 \times 10)$
                                        $= (10 \times 2) \times 10$

Commutative Property $= (2 \times 10) \times 10$

Associative Property $= 2 \times (10 \times 10)$
                                        $= 2 \times 100$
                                        $= 200$

1. Ten times any number of tens gives you that number of hundreds. Complete the steps to show 10 times 5 tens.

   $10 \times 50 = 10 \times ($ _____ $\times$ _____ $)$

   $= (10 \times$ _____ $) \times$ _____

   $= ($ _____ $\times 10) \times$ _____

   $=$ _____ $\times (10 \times$ _____ $)$

   $=$ _____ $\times$ _____

   $=$ _____

► Model a Product of Tens

Olivia wants to tile the top of a table. The table is 20 inches by 30 inches. Olivia needs to find the area of the table in inches.

2. Find the area of this 20 × 30 rectangle by dividing it into 10-by-10 squares of 100.

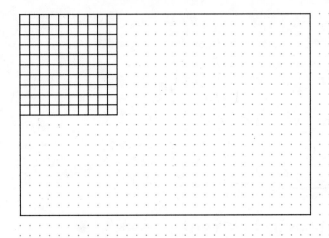

3. Each tile is a 1-inch square. How many tiles does Olivia need to cover the tabletop? _____

4. Each box of tiles contains 100 tiles. How many boxes of tiles does Olivia need to buy? _____

► Factor the Tens

5. Complete the steps to show your work in Exercise 2 numerically.

$20 \times 30 = ($ _____ $\times 10) \times ($ _____ $\times 10)$

$= ($ _____ $\times$ _____ $) \times (10 \times 10)$

$=$ _____ $\times 100$

$= 600$

6. Is it true that 20 × 30 = 30 × 20? Explain how you know.

_____

Connect Place Value and Multiplication

VOCABULARY
factor
product

▶ Look for Patterns

Multiplying greater numbers in your head is easier when you learn patterns of multiplication with tens.

Start with column A and look for the patterns used to get the expressions in each column. Copy and complete the table.

Table 1

	A	B	C	D
	2 × 3	2 × 1 × 3 × 1	6 × 1	6
1.	2 × 30	2 × 1 × 3 × 10	6 × 10	_____
2.	20 × 30	2 × 10 × 3 × 10	_____	_____

3. How are the expressions in column B different from the expressions in column A?

_____

_____

_____

4. In column C, we see that each expression can be written as a number times a place value. Which of these **factors** gives more information about the size of the **product?**

_____

5. Why is 6 the first digit of the products in column D?

_____

6. Why are there different numbers of zeros in the products in column D?

_____

_____

▶ Compare Tables

Copy and complete each table.

Table 2

	A	B	C	D
	6×3	$6 \times 1 \times 3 \times 1$	18×1	18
7.	6×30	$6 \times 1 \times 3 \times 10$	18×10	_____
8.	60×30	$6 \times 10 \times 3 \times 10$	_____	_____

Table 3

	A	B	C	D
	5×8	$5 \times 1 \times 8 \times 1$	40×1	40
9.	5×80	$5 \times 1 \times 8 \times 10$	40×10	_____
10.	50×80	_____	_____	_____

11. Why do the products in Table 2 have more digits than the products in Table 1?

_____

_____

12. Why are there more zeros in the products in Table 3 than the products in Table 2?

_____

_____

Mental Math and Multiplication

► Explore the Area Model

	20	+	6
4			

1. How many square units of area are there in the tens part of the drawing? _____

2. What multiplication equation gives the area of the tens part of the drawing? Write this equation in its rectangle.

   _____

3. How many square units of area are there in the ones part? _____

4. What multiplication equation gives the area of the ones part? Write this equation in its rectangle. _____

5. What is the total of the two areas? _____

6. How do you know that 104 is the correct product of 4×26?

   _____

7. Read problems A and B.

   A. Al's photo album has 26 pages. Each page has 4 photos. How many photos are in Al's album?

   B. Nick took 4 photos. Henri took 26 photos. How many more photos did Henri take than Nick?

   Which problem could you solve using the multiplication you just did? Explain why.

   _____

   _____

   _____

▶ Use Rectangles to Multiply

Draw a rectangle for each problem on your MathBoard.
Find the tens product, the ones product, and the total.

8. 3 × 28

9. 3 × 29

10. 5 × 30

11. 5 × 36

_____

_____

_____

12. 4 × 38

13. 8 × 38

14. 4 × 28

15. 5 × 28

_____

_____

_____

Solve each problem.

Show your work.

16. Maria's father planted 12 rows of tomatoes in his garden. Each row had 6 plants. How many tomato plants were in Maria's father's garden?

_____

17. A library subscribes to 67 magazines. Each month the library receives 3 copies of each magazine. How many magazines does the library receive each month?

_____

18. Complete this word problem. Then solve it.

_____ has _____ boxes of _____.

There are _____ _____ in each box.

How many _____ does _____

have altogether? _____

Model One-Digit by Two-Digit Multiplication

▶ Multiply One-Digit Dollar Amounts by Two-Digit Numbers

You can use your skills for multiplying a one-digit number by a two-digit number to multiply one-digit dollar amounts by two-digit numbers.

Find the exact cost. Give your answer in dollars.

Show your work.

19. A package of paper costs $2. If someone is purchasing 24 packages, how much will it cost?

_____

20. A box lunch can be purchased for $3. How much will 83 lunches cost?

_____

21. A movie ticket costs $8 per person. If 61 people go to the five o'clock show, how much money does the theater make for that show?

_____

22. A round-trip train ticket costs $4 per person. If 58 fourth-graders take a class trip to the city on the train, how much will the train tickets cost altogether?

_____

23. Admission to the zoo costs $5 per person. If a group of 72 students takes a trip to the zoo, how much will their tickets cost altogether?

_____

24. Sara earns $9 per hour as a cashier. How much does she earn in a 40-hour week?

_____

► **Multiply Two-Digit Dollar Amounts by One-Digit Numbers**

You can use your skills for multiplying a one-digit number by a two-digit number to multiply one-digit numbers by two-digit dollar amounts.

Find the exact cost. Give your answer in dollars.   *Show your work.*

25. A bike costs $53. If 2 bikes are purchased, how much will be the total cost?

   _____

26. A store sells CDs for $14. If someone buys 7 of them, how much will they cost altogether?

   _____

27. An amusement park entrance fee is $23 per person. If 4 friends go to the amusement park, how much will their tickets cost altogether?

   _____

28. A hotel costs $72 per night. How much will it cost to stay 3 nights?

   _____

29. An airplane ticket costs $87. How much will 6 tickets cost?

   _____

30. Jorge earns $99 each week. He goes on vacation in 9 weeks. How much will he earn before his vacation?

   _____

VOCABULARY
estimate
rounding

► Estimate Products

It is easier to **estimate** the product of a two-digit number and a one-digit number when you think about the two multiples of ten close to the two-digit number. This is shown in the drawings below.

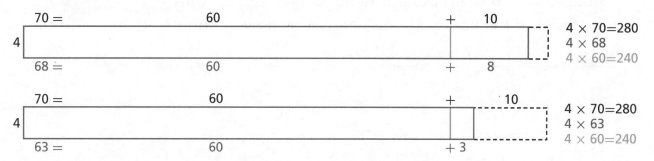

1. In each drawing, find the rectangles that represent 4 × 70 and 4 × 60. These rectangles "frame" the rectangles for 4 × 68 and 4 × 63. Find the values of 4 × 70 and 4 × 60.

   4 × 70 = _____   4 × 60 = _____

2. Look at the rectangle that represents 4 × 68. Is 4 × 68 closer to 4 × 60 or to 4 × 70? So is 4 × 68 closer to 240 or 280?

   _____

3. Look at the rectangle that represents 4 × 63. Is 4 × 63 closer to 4 × 60 or to 4 × 70? Is 4 × 63 closer to 240 or 280?

   _____

4. Explain how to use **rounding** to estimate the product of a one-digit number and a two-digit number.

   _____

   _____

   _____

▶ Practice Estimation

Discuss how rounding and estimation could help solve these problems.

5. Keesha's school has 185 fourth-grade students. The library has 28 tables with 6 chairs at each table. Can all of the fourth-graders sit in the library at one time? How do you know?

_____

_____

_____

_____

6. Ameena is printing the class newsletter. There are 8 pages in the newsletter, and she needs 74 copies. Each package of paper contains 90 sheets. How many packages of paper does she need to print the newsletter?

_____

_____

_____

_____

_____

Estimate each product. Then solve to check your estimate.

7. 3×52 _____

8. 7×48 _____

9. 9×27 _____

10. 8×34 _____

11. 8×35 _____

12. 5×22 _____

VOCABULARY
Place Value Sections Method

▶ Use the Place Value Sections Method

You can use an area model to demonstrate the
Place Value Sections Method. This strategy is
used below for multiplying a one-digit number
by a two-digit number.

Complete the steps.

$27 =$ 20   +   7

5 | $5 \times 20 = 100$ | $5 \times 7 = 35$ | 5 $+$ ___

Use the Place Value Sections Method to solve the problem.
Complete the steps.

1. The fourth-grade class is participating in a walk-a-thon.
   Each student will walk 8 laps around the track. There
   are 92 fourth-grade students. How many laps will the
   fourth-grade class walk?

   _____

   $92 =$ 90   +   2

   8 | ___ $\times$ ___ = ___ | ___ $\times$ ___ = ___ | 8 $+$ ___

Draw an area model and use the Place Value Sections
Method to solve the problem.

2. A football coach is ordering 3 shirts for each football player.
   There are 54 players in the football program. How many
   shirts does the coach need to order for the entire program?

   _____

Name _____   Date _____

VOCABULARY
Expanded Notation Method

▶ Use the Expanded Notation Method

You can also use an area model to show how to use the **Expanded Notation Method**. Use the Expanded Notation Method to solve 5 × 27 below.

Complete the steps.

3.

$$27 = \underline{\quad} + \underline{\quad}$$
$$\times\ 5 = \underline{\quad\quad}$$
$$\underline{\quad} \times \underline{\quad} = \underline{\quad}$$
$$\underline{\quad} \times \underline{\quad} = \underline{\quad}$$
$$\underline{\quad}$$

Use the Expanded Notation Method to solve the problem. Complete the steps.

4. A farm stand sold 4 bushels of apples in one day. Each bushel of apples weighs 42 pounds. How many pounds of apples did the farm stand sell?

$$42 = \quad 40 \quad + \quad 2$$

$$\underline{\quad} = \underline{\quad} + \underline{\quad}$$
$$\underline{\quad} =$$
$$\underline{\quad} \times \underline{\quad} = \underline{\quad}$$
$$\underline{\quad} \times \underline{\quad} = \underline{\quad}$$
$$\underline{\quad}$$

Draw an area model and use the Expanded Notation Method to solve the problem.

5. A marina needs to replace the boards on their pier. The pier is 7 feet by 39 feet. What is the area of the boards that need to be replaced?

_____

© Houghton Mifflin Harcourt Publishing Company

Use Place Value to Multiply

VOCABULARY
Distributive Property
partial products

▶ **Model the Distributive Property**

You have used area models to help you multiply. You can use the area model to find 3 × 74 by writing 74 in expanded form and using the **Distributive Property** to find **partial products**. After you find all the partial products, you can add them together to find the actual product of 3 × 74.

Complete each exercise.

1. Write 74 in expanded form.

   3 × 74 = 3 (_____ + _____)

2. Use the Distributive Property.

   3 × 74 = (_____ × _____) + (_____ × _____)

The area models below show the steps to find the solution to 3 × 74.

STEP 1 74 =

70	+	4

3 | 3 × 70 = 210 | | 3

Multiply the tens.

(3 × 70) = _____

STEP 2 74 =

70	+	4

3 | | 3 × 4 = 12 | 3

Multiply the ones.

(3 × 4) = _____

STEP 3 74 =

70	+	4

3 | 3 × 70 = 210 | 3 × 4 = 12 | 3

Add the   210
partial products. + 12
                  _____

3. What is the actual product of 3 × 74? _____

VOCABULARY
Algebraic Notation Method

▶ Use the Algebraic Notation Method to Multiply

Another numerical multiplication method that can be represented by an area model is the **Algebraic Notation Method**. This method also decomposes the two-digit factor into tens and ones and then uses the Distributive Property.

Use the Algebraic Notation Method to solve each problem. Complete the steps.

4. $8 \cdot 62$

62 = ____ + ____

$8 \cdot 62 = $ ____ $\cdot ($ ____ $ + $ ____ $)$
      $= 480 + 16$
      $= 496$

5. $2 \cdot 97$

97 = ____ + ____

$2 \cdot 97 = $ ____ $\cdot ($ ____ $ + $ ____ $)$
      $= 180 + 14$
      $= 194$

Draw an area model and use the Algebraic Notation Method to solve the problem.

6. There are 9 members on the school's golf team. Each golfer hit a bucket of 68 golf balls at the driving range. How many golf balls did the entire team hit?

   _____

7. What is the first step in the Algebraic Notation Method?

   _____

▶ Numerical Multiplication Methods

You have used the area model to help you multiply. In this lesson, you will compare the numerical multiplication methods that are related to this area model.

Place Value Sections Method

$37 =$ 30 $+$ 7

| 4 | $4 \times 30 = 120$ | $4 \times 7 = 28$ | 4 |

$\begin{array}{r} 120 \\ + 28 \\ \hline 148 \end{array}$

Expanded Notation Method

$37 =$ 30 $+$ 7

$\begin{array}{r} 37 = 30 + 7 \\ \times\ 4 = \qquad 4 \\ \hline 4 \times 30 = 120 \\ 4 \times\ 7 =\ \ 28 \\ \hline 148 \end{array}$

Algebraic Notation Method

$37 =$ 30 $+$ 7

$4 \times 37 = 4 \times (30 + 7)$
$\quad\quad\quad = 120 + 28$
$\quad\quad\quad = 148$

▶ Connect the Multiplication Methods

Refer to the examples above.

1. What two values are added together to give the answer in all three methods?

_____

2. What is different about the three methods?

_____

▶ Practice Different Methods

Fill in the blanks in the following solutions.

3. 4×86

Expanded Notation

$$86 = \underline{\quad} + 6$$
$$\times \ 4 = \qquad \underline{\quad}$$
$$\overline{\rule{5cm}{0.4pt}}$$
$$4 \times \underline{\quad} = \underline{\quad}$$
$$\overline{\rule{5cm}{0.4pt}}$$
$$\underline{\quad} \times 6 = 24$$
$$\overline{\rule{5cm}{0.4pt}}$$
$$\underline{\quad}$$

Algebraic Notation

$$4 \cdot 86 = \underline{\quad} \cdot (80 + 6)$$
$$= 320 + \underline{\quad}$$
$$= \underline{\quad}$$

4. 4×68

Expanded Notation

$$\underline{\quad} = 60 + 8$$
$$\times \ 4 = \qquad \underline{\quad}$$
$$\overline{\rule{5cm}{0.4pt}}$$
$$4 \times \underline{\quad} = \underline{\quad}$$
$$\overline{\rule{5cm}{0.4pt}}$$
$$\underline{\quad} \times 8 = 32$$
$$\overline{\rule{5cm}{0.4pt}}$$
$$\underline{\quad}$$

Algebraic Notation

$$4 \cdot 68 = 4 \cdot (\underline{\quad} + \underline{\quad})$$
$$= 240 + \underline{\quad}$$
$$= \underline{\quad}$$

Solve using a numerical method. Draw the related area model.

5. $5 \times 64 = \underline{\quad}$

6. $6 \times 72 = \underline{\quad}$

7. $7 \times 92 = \underline{\quad}$

8. $8 \times 53 = \underline{\quad}$

9. $5 \times 46 = \underline{\quad}$

10. $6 \times 27 = \underline{\quad}$

► Compare Multiplication Methods

Compare these methods for solving 9 × 28.

Method A	Method B	Method C	Method D
28 = 20 + 8	28 = 20 + 8	28	28
× 9 = 9	× 9 = 9	× 9	× 9
9 × 20 = 180	180	180	72
9 × 8 = 72	72	72	180
252	252	252	252

1. How are all the methods similar? List at least two similarities.

_____

_____

_____

2. How are the methods different? List at least three differences.

_____

_____

_____

Discuss how the recording methods below show the partial products in different ways.

© Houghton Mifflin Harcourt Publishing Company

▶ **Discuss the Shortcut Method**

The steps for the Shortcut Method are shown below.

Shortcut Method with New Groups Above			Shortcut Method with New Groups Below		
Method E:	**Step 1**	**Step 2**	**Method F:**	**Step 1**	**Step 2**
	$\overset{7}{28}$	$\overset{7}{28}$		28	28
	$\times\ 9$	$\times\ 9$		$\times\ 9$	$\times\ 9$
	2	252		$_{7}2$	$_{7}252$

3. Where are the products 180 and 72 from Methods A–D?

_____

_____

_____

▶ **Practice Multiplication**

Solve using any method. Sketch a rectangle if necessary.

4.   63
    × 5

5.   39
    × 8

6.   98
    × 2

7.   86
    × 4

8.   25
    × 7

9.   47
    × 9

10.   76
    × 3

11.   54
    × 6

▶ Use Rectangles to Multiply Hundreds

You can use a model to show multiplication with hundreds.
Study this model to see how we can multiply 7 × 300.

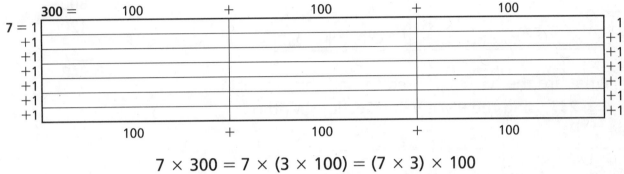

$$7 \times 300 = 7 \times (3 \times 100) = (7 \times 3) \times 100$$

$$= 21 \times 100$$

$$= 2{,}100$$

1. How many hundreds are represented in each column of the model?

   _____

2. How does knowing that 7 × 3 = 21 help you find 7 × 300?

   _____

   _____

3. What property of multiplication is used in the equation, 7 × (3 × 100) = (7 × 3) × 100?

   _____

4. Sketch a model of 6 × 400. Be ready to explain your model.

► Compare the Three Methods

You can use the **Place Value Sections Method** to multiply a one-digit number by a three-digit number.

237 =	200	+ 30	+ 7
4	4 × 200 = 800	4 × 30 = 120	4 × 7 = 28	4

$$800$$
$$120$$
$$+ \ 28$$
$$\overline{948}$$

5. What are the two steps used to find the product of 4 × 237 using the Place Value Sections Method.

_____

The **Expanded Notation Method** uses the same steps as the Place Value Sections Method.

237 =	200	+ 30	+ 7
4			4

$$237 = 200 + 30 + 7$$
$$\times 4 = \qquad\qquad 4$$
$$\overline{4 \times 200 = 800}$$
$$4 \times 30 = 120$$
$$4 \times 7 = \ \ 28$$
$$\overline{\qquad\qquad 948}$$

6. What is the last step in the Expanded Notation Method and the Place Value Sections Method?

_____

The **Algebraic Notation Method** uses expanded form just like the other two methods. Even though the steps look different, they are the same as in the other methods.

$$4 \cdot 237 = 4 \cdot (200 + 30 + 7)$$
$$= (4 \cdot 200) + (4 \cdot 30) + (4 \cdot 7)$$
$$= 800 + 120 + 28$$
$$= 948$$

7. What is the first step in all three methods?

_____

▶ Practice Multiplication

**Solve using any method. Show your work.
Draw an area model if necessary.**

8. $7 \times 321 =$ _____

9. $5 \times 218 =$ _____

10. $612 \times 2 =$ _____

11. $154 \times 6 =$ _____

12. $236 \times 4 =$ _____

13. $3 \times 273 =$ _____

14. $482 \times 9 =$ _____

15. $8 \times 615 =$ _____

► Multiplication With Dollar Amounts

You can use your skills for multiplying a one-digit number by a three-digit number to multiply one-digit dollar amounts by three-digit numbers and one-digit numbers by three-digit dollar amounts.

Find the exact cost. Give your answer in dollars.

Show your work.

16. A car tire costs $158. If Danica needs to buy new tires, how much will 4 tires cost?

_____

17. The fourth grade is going on a field trip to the planetarium. A ticket costs $6. How much will it cost if 127 people go on the field trip?

_____

18. A round-trip airplane ticket costs $224. If a group of 5 people buy tickets, how much will their tickets cost?

_____

19. A book costs a bookstore $7 to order. If the store orders 325 copies of the book, how much does the store pay for the books?

_____

20. During the summer, Joe makes $115 each week mowing lawns. How much will Joe make in 9 weeks?

_____

21. A ticket to a show costs $8. There are 540 seats in the theater. If all the seats in the theater are occupied, how much money does the theater make for that show?

_____

▶ Discuss Problems With Too Much Information

A word problem may sometimes include more information than you need. Read the following problem and then answer each question.

Mrs. Sanchez is putting a border around her garden. Her garden is a rectangle with dimensions 12 feet by 18 feet. The border material costs $3.00 per foot. How many feet of border material is needed?

1. Identify any extra numerical information. Why isn't this information needed?

   _____

   _____

2. Solve the problem. _____

Solve each problem. Cross out information that is not needed.

Show your work.

3. Judy bought a CD for $10. It has 13 songs. Each song is 3 minutes long. How long will it take to listen to the whole CD?

   _____

4. Jerry has 64 coins in his coin collection and 22 stamps in his stamp collection. His sister has 59 stamps in her collection. How many stamps do they have altogether?

   _____

5. Adrian has been playing the piano for 3 years. He practices 20 minutes a day. He is preparing for a recital that is 9 days away. How many minutes of practice will he complete before the recital?

   _____

▶ Discuss Problems With Too Little Information

When solving problems in real life, you need to determine what information is needed to solve the problem. Read the following problem and then answer each question.

The campers and staff of a day camp are going to an amusement park on a bus. Each bus holds 26 people. How many buses will be needed?

6. Do you have enough information to solve this problem? What additional information do you need?

_____

_____

Determine if the problem can be solved. If it cannot be solved, tell what information is missing. If it can be solved, solve it.

7. Richard is saving $5 a week to buy a bike. When will he have enough money?

_____

8. Natalie wants to find out how much her cat weighs. She picks him up and steps on the scale. Together, they weigh 94 pounds. How much does the cat weigh?

_____

9. Phyllis wants to make 8 potholders. She needs 36 loops for each potholder. How many loops does she need?

_____

10. For one of the problems that could not be solved, rewrite it so it can be solved and then solve it.

_____

_____

Multistep Word Problems

▶ Discuss Problems With Hidden Questions

Mrs. Norton bought 2 packages of white cheese with 8 slices in each pack. She bought 3 packages of yellow cheese with 16 slices in each pack. How many more slices of yellow cheese than white cheese did she buy?

11. What do you need to find?

_____

_____

12. What are the hidden questions?

_____

_____

13. Answer the hidden questions to solve the problem.

How many slices of white cheese? $2 \times 8 = $ _____

How many slices of yellow cheese? $3 \times 16 = $ _____

How many more slices of yellow cheese? $48 - 16 = $ _____

Read the problem. Then answer the questions.   *Show your work.*

Maurice has 6 boxes of markers. June has 5 boxes of markers. Each box contains 8 markers. How many markers do Maurice and June have altogether?

14. Write the hidden questions.

_____

_____

15. Solve the problem.

_____

_____

► Mixed Problem Solving

Solve each problem and show your work.

Show your work.

16. Mr. Collins counts 54 cartons and 5 boxes of paper clips. Each carton contains 8 boxes. A box of paper clips costs $2. How many boxes of paper clips does he have?

_____

17. Ms. Washington has 5 cartons of black printer ink. She has 4 cartons of color printer ink. Each carton contains 48 cartridges of ink. How many ink cartridges are there in all?

_____

► What's the Error?

Dear Math Students,

My school is collecting cans for the annual food drive. There are 608 students in the entire school. A can of soup costs about $1. Each student will bring in 3 cans for the food drive. I wrote this multiplication to find the number of cans the school will collect in all.

I am not sure if my answer is correct. Can you help me?

Your friend,
Puzzled Penguin

$$\begin{array}{r} \overset{2}{6}08 \\ \times\ \ \ 3 \\ \hline 1,864 \end{array}$$

18. Write a response to Puzzled Penguin.

_____

_____

_____

Multistep Word Problems

► Compare Models

A coin-collecting book holds 24 coins on a page. There are
37 pages in the book. How many coins can the book hold?
The models below all show the solution to 24 × 37.

Area Model Sketch

Place Value Sections Method

$$20 \times 30 = \mathbf{600}$$
$$20 \times 7 = \mathbf{140}$$
$$4 \times 30 = \mathbf{120}$$
$$\underline{4 \times 7 = \;\;\mathbf{28}}$$

1. Describe how each model shows 6 hundreds, 14 tens,
12 tens, and 28 ones.

_____

▶ Investigate Products in the Sketch

Complete each equation.

2. $20 \times 30 = 2 \times 10 \times 3 \times 10$
$ = 2 \times 3 \times \underline{10 \times 10}$
$ = 6 \times \underline{\hspace{1cm}}$
$ = \underline{\hspace{1cm}}$

3. $20 \times 7 = 2 \times 10 \times 7 \times 1$
$ = 2 \times 7 \times \underline{10 \times 1}$
$ = 14 \times \underline{\hspace{1cm}}$
$ = \underline{\hspace{1cm}}$

4. $4 \times 30 = 4 \times 1 \times 3 \times 10$
$ = 4 \times 3 \times \underline{1 \times 10}$
$ = 12 \times \underline{\hspace{1cm}}$
$ = \underline{\hspace{1cm}}$

5. $4 \times 7 = 4 \times 1 \times 7 \times 1$
$ = 4 \times 7 \times \underline{1 \times 1}$
$ = 28 \times \underline{\hspace{1cm}}$
$ = \underline{\hspace{1cm}}$

6. Explain how the underlined parts in Exercises 2–5 are shown in the dot drawing.

_____

_____

_____

_____

7. Find 24×37 by adding the products in Exercises 2–5.

_____

▶ Practice and Discuss Modeling

Use your MathBoard to sketch an area drawing for each exercise. Then find the product.

8. 36×58 _____

9. 28×42 _____

10. 63×27 _____

11. 26×57 _____

12. 86×35 _____

13. 38×65 _____

Name _____   Date _____

▶ Compare Multiplication Methods

Each area model is the same. Study how these three methods of recording 43 × 67 are related to the area models.

Place Value Sections Method

$$40 \times 60 = 2{,}400$$
$$40 \times 7 = 280$$
$$3 \times 60 = 180$$
$$3 \times 7 = + 21$$
$$\overline{2{,}881}$$

Expanded Notation Method

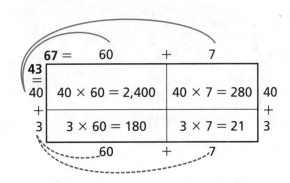

$$
\begin{array}{r}
67 (60 + 7) \\
\times\ 43 = 40 + 3 \\
\hline
40 \times 60 = 2{,}400 \\
40 \times 7 = 280 \\
3 \times 60 = 180 \\
3 \times 7 = 21 \\
\hline
2{,}881
\end{array}
$$

Algebraic Notation Method

$$43 \cdot 67 = (40 + 3) \cdot (60 + 7)$$
$$= 2{,}400 + 280 + 180 + 21$$
$$= 2{,}881$$

1. What is alike about all the three methods?

_____

_____

► Other Ways to Record Multiplication

Discuss how the recording methods below show the partial products in different ways.

Show partial products		Show new groups
67		67
× 43		× 43
21	3 × 7	¹²81
180	3 × 6 tens	²²+ 480
280	4 tens × 7	¹2,881
+ 2,400	4 tens × 6 tens	
¹2,881		

► The Shortcut Method

The steps for the Shortcut Method are shown below.

New Groups Above

Step 1	Step 2	Step 3	Step 4	Step 5
²67	²67	²²67	²²67	²²67
× 43	× 43	× 43	× 43	× 43
1	201	201	201	201
		8	268	+ 268
				2,881

New Groups Below

Step 1	Step 2	Step 3	Step 4	Step 5
67	67	67	67	67
× 43	× 43	× 43	× 43	× 43
²1	²201	²²201	²²201	²²201
		8	268	+ 268
				2,881

Discuss how the area drawing below relates to the Shortcut Method.

67

40	40 × 67 = 2,680
+ 3	3 × 67 = 201

Different Methods for Two-Digit Multiplication

▶ Estimate Products

Two-digit products can be estimated by rounding each number to the nearest ten.

Estimate and then solve.

1. 28 × 74

2. 84 × 27

3. 93 × 57

4. 87 × 54

5. 38 × 62

6. 65 × 39

7. 26 × 43

8. 59 × 96

9. 53 × 74

10. Write a multiplication word problem. Estimate the product and then solve.

11. Would using an estimate be problematic in the situation you wrote for Exercise 10? Explain why or why not.

Name _____   Date _____

▶ What's the Error?

Dear Math Students,

My friends and I are helping build flower boxes for a community garden. We are going to build 42 flower boxes. The building plans say each box needs 13 nails. I rounded to estimate how many nails we'll need. Since 40 x 10 = 400, I bought a box of 400 nails.

My friends say we won't have enough nails. Did I make a mistake? Can you help me estimate how many nails we need?

Your friend,
Puzzled Penguin

12. Write a response to Puzzle Penguin.

_____

_____

_____

Estimate and then solve. Explain whether the estimate is problematic in each situation.

13. Sally's family is taking an 18-day vacation and needs to have someone take care of their cat. A veterinarian charges $14 per day to care for the cat. How much money do they need to save to care for the cat?

_____

_____

14. An artist uses 47 tiles to make a mosaic. The artist needs to make 21 mosaics for a fair. How many tiles does the artist need to buy?

_____

_____

Check Products of Two-Digit Numbers

Name _____   **Date** _____

▶ Practice Multiplication Methods

1. Multiply 38 × 59.

Shortened Expanded Notation Method   **Shortcut Method**

$$\begin{array}{r} 38 \\ \times\ 59 \\ \hline \end{array}$$

$$\begin{array}{r} 38 \\ \times\ 59 \\ \hline \end{array}$$

Solve using any method and show your work.
Check your work with estimation.

2. 43 × 22

_____

3. 25 × 15

_____

4. 31 × 62

_____

5. 54 × 72

_____

6. 81 × 33

_____

7. 49 × 62

_____

▶ Practice Multiplication

With practice, you will be able to solve a multiplication
problem using fewer written steps.

Solve.

Show your work.

8. Between his ninth and tenth birthdays, Jimmy read
   1 book each week. There are 52 weeks in a year. If each
   book had about 95 pages, about how many pages did
   he read during the year?

   _____

9. Sam's father built a stone wall in their back yard.
   The wall was 14 stones high and 79 stones long.
   How many stones did he use to build the wall?

   _____

10. Balloon Bonanza sells party balloons in packages of
    25 balloons. There are 48 packages in the store.
    How many balloons are in 48 packages?

    _____

11. Brian is buying T-shirts for the marching band.
    He knows that at parades the band forms 24 rows.
    Each row has 13 students. If T-shirts come in boxes
    of 100, how many boxes of T-shirts should Brian buy?

    _____

▶ Use Rectangles to Multiply Thousands

You can use a model to multiply greater numbers.
Notice that each of the smaller rectangles in this model
represents one thousand. Each of the columns represents
seven one-thousands or 7,000.

$$7 \times 3,000 = 7 \times (3 \times 1,000) = (7 \times 3) \times 1,000$$
$$= 21 \times 1,000$$
$$= 21,000$$

1. While multiplying by thousands, how many zeros can
   you expect in the product?

   _____

2. How does thinking of 3,000 as 3 × 1,000 help you to
   multiply 7 × 3,000?

   _____

   _____

   _____

   _____

3. Draw a model for 4 × 8,000. Then find the product.

   _____

► Compare Multiplication Methods

You can use the multiplication methods you have learned to multiply a one-digit number times a four-digit number.

Find 8 × 3,248.

3,248 =	3,000	+	200	+	40	+	8
8							8

Place Value Sections Method

$8 \times 3{,}000 = 24{,}000$
$8 \times 200 = 1{,}600$
$8 \times 40 = 320$
$8 \times 8 = 64$
$25{,}984$

Expanded Notation Method

$3{,}248 = 3{,}000 + 200 + 40 + 8$
$\times 8 = 8$
$8 \times 3{,}000 = 24{,}000$
$8 \times 200 = 1{,}600$
$8 \times 40 = 320$
$8 \times 8 = 64$
$25{,}984$

Algebraic Notation Method

$8 \times 3{,}248 = 8 \times (3{,}000 + 200 + 40 + 8)$
$= (8 \times 3{,}000) + (8 \times 200) + (8 \times 40) + (8 \times 8)$
$= 24{,}000 + 1{,}600 + 320 + 64$
$= 25{,}984$

Make a rectangle drawing for each problem on your MathBoard. Then solve the problem using the method of your choice.

4. $3 \times 8{,}153 = $ _____

5. $4 \times 2{,}961 = $ _____

6. $6 \times 5{,}287 = $ _____

7. $7 \times 1{,}733 = $ _____

▶ Compare Methods of Multiplication

Look at the drawing and the five numerical solutions for 4 × 2,237.

2,237 =	2,000	+	200	+	30	+	7	
4								4

Method A	Method B	Method C	Method D	Method E	Method F
2,237 = 2,000 + 200 + 30 + 7	2,237 = 2,000 + 200 + 30 + 7	2,237	2,237	¹ ² 2,237	2,237
× 4 = 4	× 4 = 4	× 4	× 4	× 4	× 4
4 × 2,000 = 8,000	8,000	8,000	28	8,948	¹ ² 8,948
4 × 200 = 800	800	800	120		
4 × 30 = 120	120	120	800		
4 × 7 = 28	28	28	8,000		
8,948	8,948	8,948	8,948		

1. How are the solutions similar? List at least two ways.

_____

_____

_____

2. How are the solutions different? List at least three comparisons between methods.

_____

_____

_____

_____

_____

3. How do Methods A–D relate to the drawing? List at least two ways.

_____

_____

▶ Analyze the Shortcut Method

**Look at this breakdown of solution steps for Method E
and Method F.**

Method E			
Step 1	**Step 2**	**Step 3**	**Step 4**
$\overset{2}{2{,}237}$	$\overset{1\,2}{2{,}237}$	$\overset{1\,2}{2{,}237}$	$\overset{1\,2}{2{,}237}$
$\times\quad 4$	$\times\quad 4$	$\times\quad 4$	$\times\quad 4$
8	48	948	8,948

Method F			
Step 1	**Step 2**	**Step 3**	**Step 4**
$2{,}237$	$2{,}237$	$2{,}237$	$2{,}237$
$\times\ \underset{2}{\ \ 4}$	$\times\ \underset{1\,2}{\ \ 4}$	$\times\ \underset{1\,2}{\ \ 4}$	$\times\ \underset{1\,2}{\ \ 4}$
8	48	948	8,948

4. Describe what happens in Step 1.

_____

_____

_____

5. Describe what happens in Step 2.

_____

_____

_____

_____

6. Describe what happens in Step 3.

_____

_____

_____

7. Describe what happens in Step 4.

_____

_____

_____

▶ Round and Estimate With Thousands and Hundreds

You can use what you know about rounding and multiplication with thousands to estimate the product of 4 × 3,692.

8. Find the product if you round up: 4 × 4,000 = _____

9. Find the product if you round down: 4 × 3,000 = _____

10. Which one of the two estimates will be closer to the actual solution? Why?

    _____

11. Calculate the actual solution. _____

12. Explain why neither estimate is very close to the actual solution.

    _____

    _____

13. What would be the estimate if you added 4 × 600 to 4 × 3,000; (4 × 3,000) + (4 × 600)? _____

14. What would be the estimate if you added 4 × 700 to 4 × 3,000; (4 × 3,000) + (4 × 700)? _____

15. Estimate 4 × 7,821 by rounding 7,821 to the nearest thousand.

    _____

16. Find the actual product. _____

17. Find a better estimate for 4 × 7,821. Show your work.

    _____

    _____

Round, estimate, and fix the estimate as needed.

18. 6 × 3,095   19. 7 × 2,784

    _____   _____

    _____   _____

► Estimate Products

You can use estimation to decide if an answer is reasonable.

Solve and then estimate to check if your answer is reasonable. Show your estimate.

20. $5 \times 3{,}487 =$ _____

21. $7 \times 8{,}894 =$ _____

_____

_____

_____

_____

22. $4 \times 7{,}812 =$ _____

23. $3 \times 4{,}109 =$ _____

_____

_____

_____

_____

► What's the Error?

Dear Math Students,

My school collected 2,468 empty cartons of milk during the day today. If the school collects about the same number of cartons each day for 5 days, I estimated that the school will collect 17,500 empty cartons of milk. I wrote this estimate.

$$(5 \times 3{,}000) + (5 \times 500) = 17{,}500$$

I am not sure if this is a reasonable estimate. Can you help me?

Your Friend,
Puzzled Penguin

24. Write a response to Puzzled Penguin.

_____

_____

_____

► Practice Mixed Multiplication

Solve using any method and show your work. Check your work with estimation.

1. 35 × 9 _____

2. 56 × 17 _____

3. 228 × 2 _____

4.   23
  × 7

5.   77
  × 9

6.   59
  × 3

7.   92
  × 84

8.   49
  × 12

9.   61
  × 36

10.   459
  ×   4

11.   588
  ×   6

12.   216
  ×   7

13. 3,473
  ×   5

14. 1,156
  ×   8

15. 2,937
  ×   3

▶ Practice with Word Problems

Solve using any method and show your work.
Check your work with estimation.

Show your work.

16. The lines on a doubles tennis court are painted to be 78 feet long and 36 feet wide. The lines on a singles tennis court are painted to be 78 feet long and 27 feet wide. What is the difference between the areas of a doubles tennis court and a singles tennis court?

17. A movie theater has 287 crates of popcorn. Each crate holds 8 pounds of popcorn. There are 13 people who work at the theater. How many pounds of popcorn are there altogether?

18. Jenny goes to a 55-minute-long dance class 3 days each week. There are 9 weeks until the class recital. How many minutes of dance class are there until the recital?

19. Alex is shopping for school clothes. He buys 4 shirts for $12 each. He also buys 3 pairs of shorts for $17 each. How much does Alex spend on school clothes in all?

20. Casey draws a rectangular array that is 1,167 units long and 7 units wide. What is the area of Casey's array?

Practice Multiplying

▶ Math and Games

This is a game called *Big City Building*. The goal of the game is to design and build a successful city within a budget. To win the game, the city must have all of the features of a real-life city such as apartments, schools, parks, and shops, so its residents will be happy.

1. Each city in *Big City Building* requires a fire station, a police station, and a post office. These each cost $2,657 in taxes per year to maintain. How much does it cost to maintain the fire station, the police station, and the post office building for one year?

_____

2. In *Big City Building*, the roads are standard two-lane roads. The total width of the road is 9 meters. If each block is 82 meters long, what is the area of the road of one city block in square meters?

_____

▶ Big City Building

The table shows the cost of different features
on the *Big City Building* game. Below is Scott's
design, so far, for his city in *Big City Building*.

Item	Cost
Tree	$83 per tree
Shrub	$54 per shrub
Lake	$198 per square unit
Road	$288 per square unit
Apartment building	$9,179 per building
Any other building	$892 per square unit

Currently, Scott has $156,324 in *Big City Building* money
to create his city.

3. Scott buys 42 trees to put in the park. The trees cost
   $83 each. How much money does Scott pay for the trees?

   _____

4. Each apartment building contains 59 apartment units.
   Scott has 4 apartment buildings in his city. How many
   apartment units does Scott's city have?

   _____

5. If Scott's city is 27 units long and 19 units wide, what is
   the area of Scott's city in square units?

   _____

Name _____ **Date** _____

▶ Vocabulary

Choose the best term from the box.

1. _____ are the products of the ones, tens, hundreds, and so on in multidigit multiplication. **(Lessons 2-7)**

2. An _____ is a number close to an exact amount. **(Lesson 2-5)**

3. The _____ lets you find a number times a sum by multiplying the number by each addend and then adding the products. **(Lessons 2-7)**

▶ Concepts and Skills

4. Write the steps for finding 50 × 30 by factoring the tens. **(Lesson 2-2)**

   _____

   _____

5. Explain how you know that 10 × 60 = 600. **(Lesson 2-2)**

   _____

   _____

6. Explain how the Expanded Notation Method is similar to the Place Value Sections Method when multiplying a one-digit number by a two-digit number. **(Lesson 2-6)**

   _____

   _____

7. Use mental math to find each product. **(Lesson 2-3)**

   4 × 7 _____   4 × 700 _____

   4 × 70 _____   4 × 7,000 _____

   40 × 70 _____

Multiply using any method. Show your work.

(Lessons 2-8, 2-10, 2-14)

8. 3×68 _____

9. 5×84 _____

10. 3×506 _____

11. 9×265 _____

12. 16×50 _____

13. 12×32 _____

14. $6 \times 4,518$ _____

15. $4 \times 2,706$ _____

Estimate each product. Solve to check your estimate.
(Lessons 2-5, 2-14, 2-17)

16. 7 × 82

_____

_____

_____

17. 33 × 66

_____

_____

_____

18. 46 × 20

_____

_____

_____

19. 9 × 3,276

_____

_____

_____

▶ **Problem Solving**

Find the exact cost. (Lessons 2-4, 2-10)

20. A rental car costs $63 per day. If someone rents the car for 6 days, how much will be the total cost?

_____

21. The Adventure Club is going skating. The price of admission to the skating rink is $3 per person. If there are 214 people in the club, how much will it cost the club to skate?

_____

22. A travel agent is booking flights for a group of 9 people. If each airplane ticket costs $184, how much will their tickets cost altogether?

_____

Solve each problem. List any extra numerical information. *show your work.*
(Lesson 2-15)

23. Mariah is painting wall murals in the cafeteria. One mural is 12 feet by 28 feet. The other mural is 12 feet by 32 feet. What is the total area of the cafeteria that Mariah is painting?

_____

24. A family spent 7 hours at the zoo. They bought 2 adult tickets for $20 each and 3 child tickets for $10 each. They bought lunch for $23. How much did the tickets cost?

_____

25. **Extended Response** Sketch an area model for the product 6 × 3,243. Explain how the area model can be used to find the product. (Lesson 2-16)

_____

_____

_____

_____

_____

_____

Family Letter

Dear Family,

Your child is familiar with multiplication from earlier units. Unit 3 of *Math Expressions* extends the concepts used in multiplication to teach your child division. The main goals of this unit are to:

• Learn methods for dividing whole numbers up to four digits.

• Use estimates to check the reasonableness of answers.

• Solve problems involving division and remainders.

Your child will learn and practice techniques such as the Place Value Sections, Expanded Notation, and Digit-by-Digit methods to gain speed and accuracy in division. At first, your child will learn to use patterns and multiplication to divide. Later, your child will learn to use the methods with divisors from 2 to 9. Then your child will learn to divide when there is a zero in the quotient or dividend and to watch out for potential problems involving these situations.

Examples of Division Methods:

Place Value Sections Method	Expanded Notation Method	Digit-by-Digit Method

Your child may use whatever method he or she chooses as long as he or she can explain it. Some children like to use different methods.

Place Value Sections Method

$$60 + 6 = 66$$

$$5\overline{\smash{\big)}\begin{array}{c} 330 \\ -300 \end{array}} \quad \begin{array}{c} 30 \\ 30 \end{array}$$
$$\quad 30 \qquad 0$$

Expanded Notation Method

$$\begin{array}{r} 6 \\ 60 \end{array}\Big]66$$
$$5\overline{\smash{\big)}330}$$
$$\underline{-300}$$
$$30$$
$$\underline{-30}$$
$$0$$

Digit-by-Digit Method

$$\begin{array}{r} 66 \\ 5\overline{\smash{\big)}330} \\ \underline{-30} \\ 30 \\ \underline{-30} \\ 0 \end{array}$$

Your child will also learn to interpret remainders in the context of the problem being solved; for example, when the remainder alone is the answer to a word problem.

Finally, your child will apply this knowledge to solve mixed problems with one or more steps and using all four operations.

If you have questions or problems, please contact me.

Sincerely,
Your child's teacher

COMMON CORE

This unit includes the Common Core Standards for Mathematical Content for Numbers and Operations in Base Ten, 4.NBT.6 and all Mathematical Practices.

Estimada familia:

En unidades anteriores su niño se ha familiarizado con la multiplicación. La Unidad 3 de *Math Expressions* amplía los conceptos usados en la multiplicación para que su niño aprenda la división. Los objetivos principales de esta unidad son:

• aprender métodos para dividir números enteros de hasta cuatro dígitos.

• usar la estimación para comprobar si las respuestas son razonables.

• resolver problemas que requieran división y residuos.

Su niño aprenderá y practicará técnicas tales como las de Secciones de valor posicional, Notación extendida y Dígito por dígito, para adquirir rapidez y precisión en la división. Al principio, su niño aprenderá a usar patrones y la multiplicación para dividir. Más adelante, usará los métodos con divisores de 2 a 9. Luego, aprenderá a dividir cuando haya un cero en el cociente o en el dividendo, y a detectar problemas que pueden surgir en esas situaciones.

Ejemplos de métodos de división:

Secciones de valor posicional	Notación extendida	Dígito por dígito

$$60 + 6 = 66$$

Secciones de valor posicional:
$$5 \overline{\begin{array}{c|c} 330 & 30 \\ -300 & 30 \\ \hline 30 & 0 \end{array}}$$

Notación extendida:
$$\begin{array}{c} 6 \\ 60 \end{array}\Big] 66$$
$$5)\overline{330}$$
$$\underline{-300}$$
$$30$$
$$\underline{-30}$$
$$0$$

Dígito por dígito:
$$\begin{array}{r} 66 \\ 5)\overline{330} \\ -30 \\ \hline 30 \\ -30 \\ \hline 0 \end{array}$$

Su niño puede usar el método que elija siempre y cuando pueda explicarlo. A algunos niños les gusta usar métodos diferentes.

Su niño también aprenderá a interpretar los residuos en el contexto del problema que se esté resolviendo; por ejemplo, cuando solamente el residuo es la respuesta a un problema.

Por último, su niño aplicará este conocimiento para resolver problemas mixtos de uno o más pasos, usando las cuatro operaciones.

Si tiene alguna pregunta o comentario, por favor comuníquese conmigo.

Atentamente,
El maestro de su niño

Esta unidad incluye los Common Core Standards for Mathematical Content for Numbers and Operations in Base Ten, 4.NBT.6 and all Mathematical Practices.

VOCABULARY
divisor
quotient
dividend

▶ Division Vocabulary and Models

Although multiplication and division are inverse operations, each operation has its own language.

Multiplication Words

$$3 \leftarrow \boxed{\text{Factor}}$$
$$\times\ 4 \leftarrow$$
$$12 \leftarrow \boxed{\text{Product}}$$

$\boxed{\text{Factor}} \longrightarrow 3$
$4\overline{)12} \leftarrow \boxed{\text{Product}}$
$\underline{-\ 12}$
0

Division Words

$\boxed{\text{Divisor}}\quad 3 \leftarrow \boxed{\text{Quotient}}$
$4\overline{)12}$
$\underline{-\ 12} \leftarrow \boxed{\text{Dividend}}$
0

The models for multiplication and division are the same models.

array	**rows and columns**	**area model**

12 bottles on a table

$12 \div 3 =$ _____

$3 \times$ _____ $= 12$

12 tiles on a wall

$12 \div 3 =$ _____

$3 \times$ _____ $= 12$

___ ft

3 ft | 12 sq ft

12 square feet of carpet

$12 \div 3 =$ _____

$3 \times$ _____ $= 12$

▶ Discuss Remainders

VOCABULARY
remainder

Sometimes when you divide, some are left over. The left over amount is called the **remainder**.

If you have 14 juice boxes arranged in groups of 3, how many juice boxes will be left over?

$$
\begin{array}{r}
4R2 \\
3\overline{)14} \\
-\ 12 \\
\hline
2
\end{array}
$$

← 2 are left over.
2 is the remainder.

Compare the divisor and the remainder. The remainder must be less than the divisor.

2 < 3, so the remainder is correct.

Multiply to Check Division.
Add the remainder.

$$4 \times 3 = 12$$
$$12 + 2 = 14$$

▶ Divide with Remainders

The remainder must be less than the divisor.
If it is not, increase the quotient.

```
        3                    4 R3
    5)23                 5)23
    −15                  −20
      8 no                  3 yes
      8 > 5                 3 < 5
```

```
        8                    9 R6
    9)87                 9)87
    −72                  −81
     15 no                  6 yes
     15 > 9                 6 < 9
```

Divide with remainders.

1. $2\overline{)19}$ 2. $7\overline{)50}$ 3. $9\overline{)48}$

4. $5\overline{)48}$ 5. $6\overline{)19}$ 6. $3\overline{)25}$

Divide. Multiply to check the last problem in each row.

```
                                5 R4
7. 6)27        8. 4)30        9. 7)39         7 · 5 + 4 =
                                 − 35          35 + 4 = 39
                                  4
```

10. $8\overline{)43}$ 11. $5\overline{)26}$ 12. $9\overline{)41}$

13. $5\overline{)32}$ 14. $4\overline{)21}$ 15. $3\overline{)22}$

Divide With Remainders

▶ Multiply and Divide with Zeros

When you multiply or divide with zeros, you can see a pattern.

$4 \times 1 = 4$	$4 \div 4 = 1$	$7 \times 5 = 35$	$35 \div 7 = 5$
$4 \times 10 = 40$	$40 \div 4 = 10$	$7 \times 50 = 350$	$350 \div 7 = 50$
$4 \times 100 = 400$	$400 \div 4 = 100$	$7 \times 500 = 3,500$	$3,500 \div 7 = 500$
$4 \times 1,000 = 4,000$	$4,000 \div 4 = 1,000$	$7 \times 5,000 = 35,000$	$35,000 \div 7 = 5,000$

16. What pattern do you notice when you multiply with zeros?

_____

_____

17. What pattern do you notice when you divide with zeros?

_____

_____

Find the unknown factor. Multiply to check the division.

18. $4\overline{)320}$ $4 \cdot$ _____ $= 320$ 19. $6\overline{)420}$ $6 \cdot$ _____ $= 420$

20. $7\overline{)49}$ $7 \cdot$ _____ $= 49$ 21. $3\overline{)1,800}$ $3 \cdot$ _____ $= 1,800$

22. $5\overline{)4,500}$ $5 \cdot$ _____ $= 4,500$ 23. $9\overline{)3,600}$ $9 \cdot$ _____ $= 3,600$

24. $6\overline{)3,000}$ $6 \cdot$ _____ $= 3,000$ 25. $5\overline{)4,000}$ $5 \cdot$ _____ $= 4,000$

▶ Divide With Zeros and Remainders

Divide. Multiply to check your answer.

26. $\begin{array}{r} 300 \text{ R6} \\ 7\overline{)2{,}106} \\ -2{,}100 \\ \hline 6 \end{array}$

27. $8\overline{)643}$

28. $9\overline{)275}$

29. $2\overline{)1{,}601}$

30. $3\overline{)1{,}802}$

31. $4\overline{)2{,}803}$

32. $5\overline{)4{,}503}$

33. $6\overline{)4{,}205}$

Divide With Remainders

► Multiplying and Dividing

Complete the steps.

1. Sam divides 738 by 6. He uses the Place Value
   Sections Method and the Expanded Notation Method.

   a. Sam thinks: I'll draw the Place Value Sections that I know from
      multiplication. To divide, I need to find how many hundreds,
      tens, and ones to find the unknown factor.

   Place Value Sections Method   **Expanded Notation Method**

   __hundreds + __tens + __ones
      __00   __0   __

   | 6 | 738 | | |

   $6\overline{)738}$

   b. 6 × 100 = 600 will fit. 6 × 200 = 1,200 is too big.

   __00   +   _0   +   _

   | 6 | 738 | | |

   $6\overline{)738}$

   c. I have 138 left for the other sections.
      6 × 20 = 120 will fit. 6 × 30 = 180 is too big.

   100   +   _0   +   _

   | 6 | 738
−600
138 | 138 | |

   $$\begin{array}{r} 100 \\ 6\overline{)738} \\ -600 \\ \hline 138 \end{array}$$

   d. 6 × 3 = 18

   100   +   20   +   _   = _____

   | 6 | 738
−600
138 | 138
−120
18 | 18

0 |

   $$\begin{array}{r} 20\,] \\ 100\,] \\ 6\overline{)738} \\ -600 \\ \hline 138 \\ -120 \\ \hline 18 \end{array}$$

▶ Practice the Place Value Sections Method

Solve. Use Place Value Sections Method for division.

The sidewalk crew knows that the new sidewalk at the mall will be 3,915 square feet. It will be 9 feet wide. How long will it be? _____

$$\underline{400} + \underline{30} + \underline{5} = 435$$

9 ft	3,915 −3,600	315 −270	45 −45
	315	45	0

2. The sidewalk at the theater will be 2,748 square feet. It will be 6 feet wide. How long will it be?

_____

$$\underline{}00 + \underline{}0 + \underline{} = \underline{}$$

3. Pens are packaged in boxes of 8. The store is charged for a total of 4,576 pens. How many boxes of pens did they receive?_____

$$\underline{}00 + \underline{}0 + \underline{} = \underline{}$$

4. A factory has 2,160 erasers. They package them in groups of 5. How many packages of erasers does the factory have? _____

$$\underline{} + \underline{} + \underline{} = \underline{}$$

5. A party planner has 834 small flowers to make party favors. She will put 3 flowers in each party favor. How many party favors can she make? _____

$$\underline{} + \underline{} + \underline{} = \underline{}$$

6. An artist has 956 tiles to use in a design. He plans to arrange the tiles in group of 4 tiles. How many groups of 4 tiles can he make?

_____

$$\underline{} + \underline{} + \underline{} = \underline{}$$

► Problem Solving with 3-Digit Quotients

Solve using the Expanded Notation Method for division.

7. A toy company has 740 games to donate to different schools. Each school will receive 4 games. How many schools will receive games? _____

8. A landscape architect designs a rectangular garden that is 1,232 square feet. It is 8 feet wide. How long is the garden? _____

9. The convention center is expecting 1,434 people for an event. Since each table can seat 6 people, how many tables will the convention center need to set up? _____

10. An adult lion weighs an average of 375 pounds. A lion cub weighs an average of 3 pounds at birth. How many times more does the adult lion weigh than the lion cub weighs at birth? _____

► Practice with the Expanded Notation Method

Solve using the Expanded Notation Method for division.

11. $3\overline{)552}$ **12.** $7\overline{)851}$ **13.** $2\overline{)978}$

14. $4\overline{)979}$ **15.** $3\overline{)1,098}$ **16.** $5\overline{)2,945}$

17. $7\overline{)1,652}$ **18.** $8\overline{)4,520}$ **19.** $6\overline{)3,938}$

Relate 3-Digit Multiplication to Division

▶ 2-Digit and 4-Digit Quotients

Solve. Use the Place Value Sections and the Expanded Notation
Methods for division.

1.

$$20 + 8 = 28$$

9	252	72
	− 180	− 72
	72	0

$$9\overline{)252}$$

2.

$$\_0 + \quad = \_$$

6	162	

$$6\overline{)162}$$

3.

$$\_,000 + \quad \_00 + \quad \_0 + \quad \_ = \_\_\_$$

8	8,984			

$$8\overline{)8,984}$$

4.

$$\_,000 + \quad \_00 + \quad \_0 + \quad \_ = \_\_\_$$

3	7,722			

$$3\overline{)7,722}$$

Name _____ **Date** _____

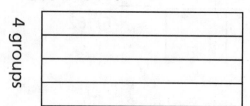

▶ Finding Group Size

5. An orchard has 516 apples ready for delivery. There are the same number of apples in each of 4 crates. How many apples are in each crate? _____

   $516 \div 4 = ?$

   4 groups

   $4)\overline{516}$

   Divide 5 hundreds, 1 ten, 6 ones equally among 4 groups.

Complete the steps.

Step 1

4 groups
1 hundred
1 hundred
1 hundred
1 hundred

5 hundreds ÷ 4

Each group gets 1 hundred.

1 hundred is left.

$$\begin{array}{r} 1 \\ 4\overline{)516} \\ -4 \\ \hline 1 \end{array}$$

Regroup 1 hundred.

10 tens + 1 ten =

11 _____

$$\begin{array}{r} 1 \\ 4\overline{)516} \\ -4 \\ \hline 11 \end{array}$$

Step 2

4 groups
1 hundred + 2 tens
1 hundred + 2 tens
1 hundred + 2 tens
1 hundred + 2 tens

11 tens ÷ 4

Each group gets 2 tens.

3 _____ are left.

$$\begin{array}{r} 12 \\ 4\overline{)516} \\ -4 \\ \hline 11 \\ -8 \\ \hline 3 \end{array}$$

Regroup 3 tens.

30 ones + 6 ones =

_____ ones

$$\begin{array}{r} 12 \\ 4\overline{)516} \\ -4 \\ \hline 11 \\ -8 \\ \hline 36 \end{array}$$

Step 3

4 groups
1 hundred + 2 tens + 9
1 hundred + 2 tens + 9
1 hundred + 2 tens + 9
1 hundred + 2 tens + 9

36 ones ÷ 4

Each group gets 9 ones.

There are _____ ones left.

$$\begin{array}{r} 129 \\ 4\overline{)516} \\ -4 \\ \hline 11 \\ -8 \\ \hline 36 \\ -36 \\ \hline 0 \end{array}$$

There are _____ apples in each crate.

Discuss 2-Digit and 4-Digit Quotients

► **Practice**

Divide.

6. $4\overline{)868}$ 7. $6\overline{)5,142}$ 8. $3\overline{)4,395}$

9. $4\overline{)332}$ 10. $7\overline{)1,617}$ 11. $7\overline{)939}$

12. $2\overline{)4,276}$ 13. $6\overline{)2,576}$ 14. $7\overline{)441}$

15. $9\overline{)3,735}$ 16. $7\overline{)406}$ 17. $3\overline{)9,954}$

▶ Division Word Problems

Solve.

Show your work.

18. What is the length of a rectangle with an area of 756 square centimeters and a width of 4 centimeters?

	?
4	756

_____

19. At a county fair, there are 7 booths that sell raffle tickets. In one day, 4,592 tickets were sold. Each booth sold the same number of tickets. How many tickets did each booth sell?

_____

20. One part of a city football stadium has 5,688 seats. The seats are arranged in 9 sections. Each section has the same number of seats. How many seats are in each section?

_____

21. An art museum has a total of 475 paintings hanging in 5 different viewing rooms. If each room has the same number of paintings, how many paintings are in each room?

_____

22. A parking garage can hold a total of 762 cars. The same number of cars can park on each floor. There are 6 floors. How many cars can park on each floor?

_____

► The Digit-by-Digit Method

1. Suppose Judith wants to divide 948 by 4. She knows how to use the Place Value Sections Method and the Expanded Notation Method, but she doesn't want to write all the zeros.

Place Value Sections Method

$$200 + \quad 30 + \quad 7 \ = 237$$

	948	148	28
4	− 800	− 120	− 28
	148	28	0

Expanded Notation Method

```
        7  ⎤
       30  ⎥ 237
      200  ⎦
    4)948
    − 800
      148
    − 120
       28
    −  28
        0
```

Judith thinks: I'll look at the place values in decreasing order. I'll imagine zeros in the other places, but I don't need to think about them until I'm ready to divide in that place.

Step 1: Look at the greatest place value first. Divide the hundreds. Then subtract.

9 hundreds ÷ 4 = 2 hundreds

```
        2
    4)948
     − 8
       1
```

Step 2: Bring down the 4. Divide the tens. Then subtract.

14 tens ÷ 4 = 3 tens

```
       23
    4)948
     − 8↓
       14
     − 12
        2
```

Step 3: Bring down the 8. Divide the ones. Then subtract.

28 ones ÷ 4 = 7 ones

```
      237
    4)948
     − 8↓
       14
     − 12↓
       28
     − 28
        0
```

► What's the Error?

Dear Math Students,

Here is a division problem I tried to solve.

```
      5,796
   3)1,738
     -15
      ‾‾‾
       23
      -21
      ‾‾‾
       28
      -27
      ‾‾‾
       18
      -18
      ‾‾‾
        0
```

Is my answer correct? If not, please help me understand why it is wrong.

Thank you,
Puzzled Penguin

2. Write a response to Puzzled Penguin.

_____

_____

_____

Solve. Use the Digit-by-Digit Method.

3. 4)3,036   **4.** 7)5,292   **5.** 6)853

Digit-by-Digit Method

► Practice

Divide.

6. 5)965

7. 8)128

8. 8)928

9. 3)716

10. 4)4,596

11. 4)982

12. 3)6,342

13. 8)578

14. 5)1,155

15. 6)3,336

16. 7)672

17. 3)4,152

▶ Solve Division Problems

Write an equation to represent the problem. Then, solve.

Show your work.

18. What is the length of a rectangle with an area of 528 square centimeters and a width of 6 centimeters?

? cm

6 cm   528 sq cm

_____

19. A cookbook features 414 recipes. There are 3 recipes on each page. How many pages are in the cookbook?

_____

20. A bus travels its route around a city once a day for 5 days. At the end of the 5th day, the bus had traveled 435 miles. How many miles did the bus travel each day?

_____

21. Ms. Tyler places a container of marbles at each table of 6 students. The students are told to share the marbles equally with the students at their table. If there are 714 marbles in the container, how many marbles should each student get?

_____

22. Sam's Used Bookstore is organizing their books on display shelves. They have 976 books and want 8 books displayed on each shelf. How many shelves will the books fill?

_____

► Compare Methods

Ellie, José, and Wanda each use their favorite method to solve 1,194 ÷ 5. Discuss the methods.

Ellie's Place Value Sections Method	José's Expanded Notation Method	Wanda's Digit-by-Digit Method

Ellie's Place Value Sections Method:

$$200 + 30 + 8 = 238 \text{ R4}$$

$$5 \begin{array}{|c|c|c|} \hline 1{,}194 & 194 & 44 \\ -1{,}000 & -150 & -40 \\ \hline 194 & 44 & 4 \end{array}$$

José's Expanded Notation Method:

$$\begin{array}{r} 8 \\ 30 \\ 200 \end{array} \Big] 238 \text{ R4}$$

$$5\overline{)1{,}194}$$
$$\underline{-1{,}000}$$
$$194$$
$$\underline{-150}$$
$$44$$
$$\underline{-40}$$
$$4$$

Wanda's Digit-by-Digit Method:

$$238 \text{ R4}$$
$$5\overline{)1{,}194}$$
$$\underline{-1\ 0}$$
$$19$$
$$\underline{-15}$$
$$44$$
$$\underline{-40}$$
$$4$$

Use any method to solve.

1. 3,248 ÷ 5 = _____

2. 5,847 ÷ 6 = _____

Solve. Use any method.

3. $5\overline{)8{,}435}$ 4. $3\overline{)2{,}604}$ 5. $4\overline{)6{,}738}$ 6. $5\overline{)9{,}714}$

Name _____   Date _____

▶ Division Practice

Use any method to solve.

7. $6\overline{)2,238}$ 8. $5\overline{)2,431}$ 9. $7\overline{)2,198}$ 10. $8\overline{)2,512}$

11. $4\overline{)5,027}$ 12. $5\overline{)5,624}$ 13. $9\overline{)3,631}$ 14. $6\overline{)6,305}$

▶ What's the Error?

Dear Math Students,

This is a problem from my math homework.
My teacher says my answer is not correct,
but I can't figure out what I did wrong.
Can you help me find and fix my mistake?

Your Friend,
Puzzled Penguin

$$
\begin{array}{r}
7{,}069 \text{ R2} \\
5\overline{)3{,}847} \\
-35 \\
\hline
34 \\
-30 \\
\hline
47 \\
-45 \\
\hline
2
\end{array}
$$

15. Write a response to Puzzled Penguin.

_____

_____

_____

_____

Relate Three Methods

▶ Practice Division

Use any method to solve.

1. 8)960

2. 4)632

3. 7)809

4. 5)736

5. 4)3,068

6. 3)6,206

7. 2)6,476

8. 6)8,825

▶ Solve Division Word Problems

Solve.

9. A helper in the school store suggests selling notebooks in packages of 4. How many packages of 4 can be made from 192 notebooks?

_____

10. Another helper suggests selling notebooks in packages of 6. How many packages of 6 can be made from 192 notebooks?

_____

11. The store will sell packages of notebooks for $3.00 each.

   a. Which would be a better deal for students, packages of 4 or packages of 6?

   _____

   _____

   b. Which package size would make more money for the store?

   _____

   _____

▶ Solve Division Word Problems (continued)

Another helper in the school store suggests making
packages of 7 or 8 notebooks.

Show your work.

12. How many packages of 7 notebooks can be made
from 896 notebooks?

_____

13. How many packages of 8 notebooks can be made
from 896 notebooks?

_____

14. The store will sell packages of notebooks for $6.00 each.

  a. Would you rather buy a package with 7 notebooks
     or a package with 8 notebooks? Explain.

  _____

  _____

  b. Would packages of 7 notebooks or packages of
     8 notebooks make more money for the store? Explain.

  _____

  _____

15. The students at Walnut Street School collected 2,790 cans
    for a recycling center. Each student brought in 5 cans.
    How many students attend the school?

_____

16. A cube can be made from 6 square cards that are
    each the same size. How many cubes can be made
    out of 7,254 cards?

_____

17. There are 5,896 beads in a barrel at a factory. These
    beads will be sold in packets of 4. How many full packets
    can be made from the beads in the barrel?

_____

Divide by Any Method

▶ What's the Error?

Dear Math Students,

The Puzzled Penguin started to solve this division problem and realized there was a problem. Some friends suggested different ways to fix it.

Your friend,
Puzzled Penguin

$$\begin{array}{r} 7 \\ 4\overline{)3,476} \\ -28 \\ \hline 6 \end{array}$$

Jacob suggested that Puzzled Penguin erase the 7 and write 8 in its place. Puzzled Penguin would also need to erase the calculations and do them over. $$\begin{array}{r} 8 \\ 4\overline{)3,476} \\ -32 \\ \hline 2 \end{array}$$	Fred told Puzzled Penguin to cross out the 7 and write 8 above it. The next step would be to subtract one more 4. $$\begin{array}{r} 8 \\ \cancel{7} \\ 4\overline{)3,476} \\ -28 \\ \hline 6 \\ -4 \end{array}$$
Amad showed Puzzled Penguin how to use the Expanded Notation Method and just keep going. $$\begin{array}{r} 100 \\ 700 \\ 4\overline{)3,476} \\ -2,800 \\ \hline 676 \\ -400 \\ \hline 276 \end{array}$$	Kris showed Puzzled Penguin how, with the Place Value Sections Method, another section can be added. $$\begin{array}{c c|c} & 700\;+ & 100 \\ \hline 4 & 3,476 & 676 \\ & -2,800 & -400 \\ \hline & 676 & 276 \end{array}$$

1. What was Puzzled Penguin's problem?

_____

2. Discuss the solutions above. Which friend was right?

_____

► Zeros in Quotients

Solve.

3. $6\overline{)1,842}$ 4. $8\overline{)5,125}$ 5. $4\overline{)4,152}$ 6. $5\overline{)9,522}$

7. $3\overline{)7,531}$ 8. $2\overline{)4,018}$ 9. $4\overline{)8,200}$ 10. $7\overline{)9,102}$

11. Cameron has a collection of 436 miniature cars that he displays on 4 shelves in a bookcase. If the cars are divided equally among the shelves, how many cars are on each shelf?

Show your work.

_____

12. The Tropical Tour Company has 2,380 brochures to distribute equally among its 7 resort hotels. How many brochures will each hotel receive?

_____

13. A factory packs 8,440 bottles of water in boxes each day. If each box contains 8 bottles, how many full boxes of water can the factory pack in one day?

_____

► Check Quotients With Rounding and Estimation

Rounding and estimating can be used to check answers.
Review your rounding skills, and then apply what you know
to division problems.

**Use rounding and estimating to decide whether each
quotient makes sense.**

1. $3\overline{)56}$ 18 R2

2. $5\overline{)463}$ 92 R3

3. $6\overline{)5,568}$ 928

4. $7\overline{)907}$ 129 R4

► Practice Dividing and Estimating

**Solve, using any method. Then check your answer by
rounding and estimating.**

5. $3\overline{)29}$

6. $6\overline{)34}$

7. $7\overline{)59}$

8. $3\overline{)72}$

9. $6\overline{)83}$

10. $7\overline{)88}$

11. $7\overline{)628}$

12. $8\overline{)683}$

13. $9\overline{)717}$

14. $7\overline{)805}$

15. $8\overline{)869}$

16. $9\overline{)914}$

17. $6\overline{)1,723}$

18. $2\overline{)2,986}$

19. $7\overline{)8,574}$

20. $6\overline{)4,652}$

21. $2\overline{)5,235}$

22. $7\overline{)7,310}$

► Estimate or Exact Answer

Some problems require an exact answer. Others require an estimate only.

Exact Answer If a problem asks for an exact answer, then you will have to do the calculation.	**Estimate** If a problem asks for a close answer and uses *about, approximately, almost,* or *nearly,* then you can estimate.
Example: The school cafeteria prepares 3,210 lunches each week. The same numbers of lunches are prepared 5 days each week. How many lunches are prepared each day?	**Example:** Milo has to read a 229-page book. He has 8 days to finish it. About how many pages should he read each day?
Discuss why you think this problem requires an exact answer.	Discuss why an estimate, and not an exact answer, is appropriate.

Decide whether you need an exact answer or an estimate. Then find the answer.

23. Sam bought a board that was 72 inches long to make bookshelves. He wants to cut the board into three equal pieces and use each one for a shelf. How long will each shelf be?

_____

24. Carl's mother baked 62 mini muffins for his class. There are 18 people in Sam's class, including the teacher. About how many mini muffins should each person get?

_____

25. Each 24-inch shelf can hold about 10 books. Approximately how many inches wide is each book?

_____

26. Malcom wants to buy 3 concert tickets. Each ticket costs $45. How much money will he need?

_____

▶ Different Kinds of Remainders

Remainders in division have different meanings, depending upon the type of problem you solve.

$$\begin{array}{r} 2\ \text{R1} \\ 4\overline{)9} \\ -8 \\ \hline 1 \end{array}$$

The same numeric solution shown at the right works for the following five problems. Discuss why the remainder means something different in each problem.

A. **The remainder is not part of the question.** Thomas has one 9-foot pine board. He needs to make 4-foot shelves for his books. How many shelves can he cut?

_____

_____

_____

B. **The remainder causes the answer to be rounded up.** Nine students are going on a field trip. Parents have offered to drive. If each parent can drive 4 students, how many parents need to drive?

_____

_____

_____

C. **The remainder is a fractional part of the answer.** One Monday Kim brought 9 apples to school. She shared them equally among herself and 3 friends. How many apples did each person get?

_____

_____

_____

_____

D. **The remainder is a decimal part of the answer.** Raul bought 4 toy cars for $9.00. Each car costs the same amount. How much did each car cost?

_____

_____

_____

E. **The remainder is the only part needed to answer the question.** Nine students have signed up to run a relay race. If each relay team can have 4 runners, how many students cannot run in the race?

_____

_____

▶ Discuss Real World Division Problems

Solve. Then discuss the meaning of the remainder.

1. Maddie tried to divide 160 stickers equally among herself and 5 friends. There were some stickers left over, so she kept them. How many stickers did Maddie get?

2. Kendra bought a bag of 200 cheese crackers for her class. If each student gets 7 crackers, how many students are there? How many crackers are left over?

3. Jerry bought shelves to hold the 132 DVDs in his collection. Each shelf can fit 8 DVDs. How many full shelves will Jerry have?

4. Racheed had 87 pennies. He divided them equally among his 4 sisters. How many pennies did Racheed have left after he gave his sisters their shares?

5. Mara wants to buy some new pencil boxes for her pencil collection. She has 47 pencils. If each pencil box holds 9 pencils, how many pencil boxes does Mara need to buy?

6. Henry's coin bank holds only nickels. Henry takes $4.42 to the bank to exchange for nickels only. How many nickels will he get from the bank?

▶ Mixed One-Step Word Problems

The fourth- and fifth-grade classes at Jackson Elementary School held a Just-for-Fun Winter Carnival. All of the students in the school were invited.

Discuss what operation you need to use to solve each problem. Then solve the problem.

1. Two students from each fourth- and fifth-grade class were on the planning committee. If Jackson School has 14 fourth- and fifth-grade classes in all, how many students planned the carnival?

2. To advertise the carnival, students decorated 4 hallway bulletin boards. They started with 2,025 pieces of colored paper. When they finished, they had 9 pieces left. How many pieces of paper did they use?

3. The parents ordered pizzas to serve at the carnival. Each pizza was cut into 8 slices. How many pizzas had to be ordered so that 1,319 people could each have one slice?

4. There were 825 students signed up to run in timed races. If exactly 6 students ran in each race, how many races were there?

5. At the raffle booth, 364 fourth-graders each bought one ticket to win a new school supply set. Only 8 fifth-graders each bought a ticket. How many students bought raffle tickets altogether?

6. Altogether, 1,263 students were enrolled in the first through fifth grades at Jackson School. On the day of the carnival, 9 students were absent. How many students could have participated in the carnival activities?

► Mixed Multistep Word Problems

Solve these problems about Pine Street School's Olympic Games.

7. At the start of the games, 193 fourth-graders signed up to play in three events. Eighty-seven played in the first event. The rest of the students were evenly divided between the second and third events. How many students played in the third event?

8. Three teams stacked paper cups into pyramids. Each team had 176 cups to use. Team 1 used exactly half of their cups. Team 2 used four times as many cups as Team 3. Team 3 used 32 cups. Which team stacked the most cups?

9. The Parents' Club provided 357 celery sticks, 676 carrot sticks, and 488 apple slices. If each student was given 3 snack pieces, how many students got a snack?

10. Seventy-five first-graders and 84 second-graders skipped around the gym. After a while, only 8 students were still skipping. How many students had stopped skipping?

11. A team from each school had 250 foam balls and a bucket. The Jackson team dunked 6 fewer balls than the Pine Street team. The Pine Street team dunked all but 8 of their balls. How many balls did the two teams dunk in all?

12. When the day was over, everybody had earned at least 1 medal, and 32 students each got 2 medals. In all, 194 each of gold, silver, and bronze medals were given out. How many students played in the games?

▶ Math and Amusement Parks

There are many things to do at an Amusement Park: ride the rides, play some games, try new foods. Many people like to ride roller coasters while at the Amusement Park.

The tallest roller coaster in the world is 456 feet tall and is located in Jackson, New Jersey. In fact, the top three tallest roller coasters in the world are in the United States.

The fourth and fifth grade classes went on a field trip to the Amusement Park.

1. There are 58 fourth grade students who are in line to ride the Loop-the-Loop roller coaster. Each roller coaster car holds 4 people. How many roller coaster cars are needed so they all can ride the roller coaster once?

Show your work.

_____

2. There are 41 fifth grade students who are in line to ride the Mile Long wooden roller coaster. Each roller coaster car holds 6 people. How many students will be in a roller coaster car that is not full?

_____

► **More Amusement Park Fun**

After riding the roller coasters, the fourth and fifth grade classes spend the rest of the day getting lunch, going shopping, and riding the rest of the rides at the Amusement Park.

Solve.

Show your work.

3. There are 27 students in Evan's group. Each student decides to get a kids meal for lunch at the food stand. If each kids meal is $7, how much did the students spend in lunch altogether?

_____

4. Thirty-one students are in line to ride the Ferris wheel. Four students are needed to fill each Ferris wheel car. How many Ferris wheel cars will be full?

_____

5. In the souvenir shop, a worker opens a box of posters. The posters in the box are bundled in groups of 8. There are a total of 2,864 posters in a box. How many bundles of posters are in the box?

_____

VOCABULARY
dividend
divisor
remainder
quotient

▶ Vocabulary

Choose the best term from the box.

1. A _____ is an answer to a division problem.
   (Lesson 3-1)

2. The number 7 is the _____ in the division problem
   548 ÷ 7. **(Lesson 3-1)**

3. In the division problem 548 ÷ 7, the number 548 is the _____.
   (Lesson 3-1)

▶ Concepts and Skills

4. List the three methods suggested in this Unit for solving division
   problems. Which division method would you use to solve 728 ÷ 6?
   Explain why you chose that method and how you would use it to
   solve the problem. **(Lessons 3-2, 3-3, 3-4, 3-5)**

   _____

   _____

5. Explain why you need to write a zero in the tens place of the
   quotient when you divide 829 by 4. **(Lesson 3-7)**

   _____

   _____

   _____

   _____

6. For what types of real world division problems might you use the
   quotient alone? When might you use only the remainder? **(Lesson 3-9)**

   _____

   _____

**Use rounding and estimation to decide whether each quotient
makes sense. (Lesson 3-8)**

7. $6\overline{)297}$ 49 R3

8. $4\overline{)3,256}$ 814

9. $8\overline{)4,229}$ 528 R5

Use any method to solve. (Lessons 3-1, 3-2, 3-3, 3-4, 3-5, 3-6, 3-7)

10. $4\overline{)716}$ 11. $9\overline{)959}$ 12. $3\overline{)6,243}$ 13. $7\overline{)940}$

14. $4\overline{)2,203}$ 15. $7\overline{)8,659}$ 16. $5\overline{)7,534}$ 17. $6\overline{)9,915}$

▶ Problem Solving

Solve.

18. There are 185 students going to a museum. Each van can hold
    9 students. How many vans of 9 students will there be? How many
    students will ride in a van that is not full? **Lesson 3-9**

19. Joshua pulls 52 loads of sand on his wagon to make a play area.
    He pulls 21 pounds of sand on each load. How many pounds of
    sand does Joshua use to make a play area? **Lesson 3-10**

20. **Extended Response** Kayla and her father baked 256 banana
    nut muffins and 298 chocolate chip muffins to sell at their
    family restaurant. They plan to place the muffins in boxes that
    hold 6 muffins each. What is the greatest number of boxes that
    can be filled with muffins? Explain how you found your answer.
    Lessons 3-9, 3-10

Dear Family,

In Unit 4 of Math Expressions, your child will apply the skills he or she has learned about operations with whole numbers while solving real world problems involving addition, subtraction, multiplication, and division.

Your child will simplify and evaluate expressions. Parentheses will be introduced to show which operation should be done first. The symbols "=" and "≠" will be used to show whether numbers and expressions are equal.

Other topics of study in this unit include situation and solution equations for addition and subtraction, as well as multiplication and division. Your child will use situation equations to represent real world problems and solution equations to solve the problems. This method of representing a problem is particularly helpful when the problems contain greater numbers and students cannot solve mentally.

Your child will also solve multiplication and addition comparison problems and compare these types of problems identifying what is the same or different.

Addition Comparison	Multiplication Comparison
Angela is 14 years old. She is 4 years older than Damarcus. How old is Damarcus?	Shawn colored 5 pages in a coloring book. Anja colored 4 times as many pages as Shawn colored. How many pages did Anja color?

Students learn that in the addition problem they are adding 4, while in the multiplication problem, they are multiplying by 4.

Your child will apply this knowledge to solve word problems using all four operations and involving one or more steps.

Finally, your child will find factor pairs for whole numbers and generate and analyze numerical and geometric patterns.

If you have any questions or comments, please call or write to me.

Sincerely,
Your child's teacher

COMMON CORE

This unit includes the Common Core Standards for Mathematical Content for Operations and Algebraic Thinking 4.OA.1, 4.OA.2, 4.OA.3, 4.OA.4, 4.OA.5, Number and Operations in Base Ten 4.NBT.4, 4.NBT.5, 4.NBT.6, Measurement and Data 4.MD.2, and all Mathematical Practices.

Estimada familia:

En la Unidad 4 de Math Expressions, su hijo aplicará las destrezas relacionadas con operaciones de números enteros que ha adquirido, resolviendo problemas cotidianos que involucran suma, resta, multiplicación y división.

Su hijo simplificará y evaluará expresiones. Se introducirán los paréntesis como una forma de mostrar cuál operación deberá completarse primero. Los signos "=" y "≠" se usarán para mostrar si los números o las expresiones son iguales o no.

Otros temas de estudio en esta unidad incluyen ecuaciones de situación y de solución para la suma y resta, así como para la multiplicación y división. Su hijo usará ecuaciones de situación para representar problemas de la vida cotidiana y ecuaciones de solución para resolver esos problemas. Este método para representar problemas es particularmente útil cuando los problemas involucran números grandes y los estudiantes no pueden resolverlos mentalmente.

Su hijo también resolverá problemas de comparación de multiplicación y suma, y comparará este tipo de problemas para identificar las semejanzas y diferencias.

Comparación de suma	Comparación de multiplicación
Ángela tiene 14 años. Ella es 4 años mayor que Damarcus. ¿Cuántos años tiene Damarcus?	Shawn coloreó 5 páginas de un libro. Ana coloreó 4 veces ese número de páginas. ¿Cuántas páginas coloreó Ana?

Los estudiantes aprenderán que en el problema de suma están sumando 4, mientras que en el problema de multiplicación, están multiplicando por 4.

Su hijo aplicará estos conocimientos para resolver problemas de uno o más pasos usando las cuatro operaciones.

Finalmente, su hijo hallará pares de factores para números enteros y generará y analizará patrones numéricos y geométricos.

Si tiene alguna pregunta por favor comuníquese conmigo.

Atentamente,
El maestro de su niño

© Houghton Mifflin Harcourt Publishing Company

COMMON CORE

Esta unidad incluye los Common Core Standards for Mathematical Content for Operations and Algebraic Thinking 4.OA.1, 4.OA.2, 4.OA.3, 4.OA.4, 4.OA.5, Number and Operations in Base Ten 4.NBT.4, 4.NBT.5, 4.NBT.6, Measurement and Data 4.MD.2, and all Mathematical Practices.

Properties and Algebraic Notation

▶ Properties and Algebraic Notation

An **expression** is one or more numbers, variables, or numbers and variables with one or more operations.	An **equation** is a statement that two expressions are equal. It has an equal sign.
Examples: 4 $6x$ $6x - 5$ $7 + 4$	Examples: $40 + 25 = 65$ $(16 \div 4) - 3 = 1$

We **simplify** an expression or equation by performing operations to combine like **terms**.

Use the Identity Property to simplify each expression.

1. $n + 5n =$ _____   2. $17t + t =$ _____   3. $x + 245x =$ _____

4. $9e - e =$ _____   5. $8c + c + c =$ _____   6. $(5z - z) - z =$ _____

Solve.

7. $30 \div (35 \div 7) =$ _____   8. $(72 \div 9) \div 4 =$ _____

9. $80 \div (32 \div 8) =$ _____   10. $13 - (9 - 1) =$ _____

11. $(600 - 400) - 10 =$ _____   12. $100 - (26 - 6) =$ _____

Use properties to find the value of ▢ or a.

13. $49 + 17 = ▢ + 49$ 14. $(a \cdot 2) \cdot 3 = 4 \cdot (2 \cdot 3)$ 15. $▢ \cdot 6 = 6 \cdot 8$

   $▢ =$ _____ $a =$ _____ $▢ =$ _____

16. $6 \cdot (40 + a) = (6 \cdot 40) + (6 \cdot 5)$ 17. $(▢ \cdot 5) + (▢ \cdot 9) = 7 \cdot (5 + 9)$

   $a =$ _____ $▢ =$ _____

18. $29 + 8 = ▢ + 29$ ⟶ Is $▢ = 4 + 2$ or $4 \cdot 2$? _____

19. $a \cdot 14 = 14 \cdot 15$ ⟶ Is $a = 5 \cdot 3$ or $5 + 3$? _____

20. $60 + 10 = ▢ + 60$ ⟶ Is $▢ = 2 + 5$ or $2 \cdot 5$? _____

▶ Parentheses in Equations

Solve.

21. $9 \cdot n = 144$

$n = $ _____

22. $s + 170 = 200$

$s = $ _____

23. $105 \div h = 7$

$h = $ _____

24. $(10 - 4) \cdot 7 = \square \cdot 7$

$\square = $ _____

25. $4 \cdot (9 - 3) = g$

$g = $ _____

26. $(10 - 6) \div 2 = b$

$b = $ _____

27. $9 \cdot (6 + 2) = \square \cdot 8$

$\square = $ _____

28. $\square \cdot 6 = 96$

$\square = $ _____

29. $(15 \div 3) \cdot (4 + 1) = v$

$v = $ _____

30. $(12 - 5) - (12 \div 6) = $ _____

31. $(23 + 4) \div (8 - 5) = $ _____

32. $(24 \div 3) \cdot (12 - 7) = $ _____

33. $(22 + 8) \div (17 - 11) = $ _____

▶ Substitute a Value

To **evaluate** an expression or equation:

1) Substitute the value of each letter.

2) Then simplify the expression by performing the operations.

Evaluate each expression.

34. $a = 4$

$19 - (a + 6)$

_____

35. $a = 10$

$(80 \div a) - 5$

_____

36. $b = 3$

$(8 \div 4) \cdot (7 - b)$

_____

37. $b = 7$

$21 \div (b - 4)$

_____

38. $b = 11$

$(b + 9) \div (7 - 2)$

_____

39. $c = 8$

$(20 - 10) + (7 + c)$

_____

40. $x = 9$

$16 \cdot (13 - x)$

_____

41. $d = 3$

$(24 \div 3) \cdot (d + 7)$

_____

42. $d = 0$

$(63 \div 7) \cdot d$

_____

VOCABULARY
sum
difference

▶ Discuss the = and ≠ Signs

An equation is made up of two equal quantities or expressions. An equal sign (=) is used to show that the two sides of the equation are equal.

$$5 = 3 + 2 \qquad 3 + 2 = 5 \qquad 5 = 5 \qquad 3 + 2 = 2 + 3 \qquad 7 - 2 = 1 + 1 + 3$$

The "is not equal to" sign (≠) shows that two quantities are not equal.

$$4 \neq 3 + 2 \qquad 5 \neq 3 - 1 \qquad 5 \neq 4 \qquad 3 - 2 \neq 1 + 3 \qquad 3 + 2 \neq 1 + 1 + 2$$

An equation can have one or more numbers or letters on each side of the equal sign. A **sum** or **difference** can be written on either side of the equal sign.

1. Use the = sign to write four equations. Vary how many numbers you have on each side of your equations.

_____   _____

_____   _____

2. Use the ≠ sign to write four "is not equal to" statements. Vary how many numbers you have on each side of your statements.

_____   _____

_____   _____

Write = or ≠ to make each statement true.

3. $5 + 2 + 6$ ___ $6 + 7$ 4. 80 ___ $60 - 20$ 5. 70 ___ $40 + 30$

6. $18 - 4 + 11$ ___ 3 7. 50 ___ $55 - (10 + 5)$ 8. $21 + 6 - 3$ ___ $26 - 4 + 2$

▶ Discuss Inverse Operations

When you add, you put two groups together. When you subtract, you find an unknown addend or take away one group from another. Addition and subtraction are inverse operations. They undo each other.

Addends are numbers that are added to make a sum. You can find two addends for a sum by breaking apart the number.

A break-apart drawing can help you find all eight related addition and subtraction equations for two addends.

$81 = 72 + 9$	$72 + 9 = 81$
$81 = 9 + 72$	$9 + 72 = 81$
$72 = 81 - 9$	$81 - 9 = 72$
$9 = 81 - 72$	$81 - 72 = 9$

9. Which equations show the Commutative Property?

_____

10. What is the total in each equation? Where is the total in a subtraction equation?

_____

Solve each equation.

11. $50 = 30 + p$

$p = $ _____

12. $q + 20 = 60$

$q = $ _____

13. $90 - v = 50$

$v = $ _____

14. Write the eight related addition and subtraction equations for the break-apart drawing.

_____   _____

_____   _____

_____   _____

_____   _____

VOCABULARY
situation equation
solution equation

▶ Write Equations to Solve Problems

A situation equation shows the structure of the information in a problem. A solution equation shows the operation that can be used to solve a problem.

Show your work.

Write an equation to solve the problem. Draw a model if you need to.

15. In a collection of 2,152 coins, 628 coins are pennies. How many coins are not pennies?

_____

_____

16. Susanna took $3,050 out of her bank account. Now she has $11,605 left in the account. How much money was in Susanna's account to start?

_____

_____

17. In the month of May, Movieland rented 563 action movies and 452 comedy movies. How many action and comedy movies in all did Movieland rent in May?

_____

_____

▶ Practice Solving Problems

Write an equation to solve the problem. Draw a model if you need to.

18. The workers at a factory made 3,250 pink balloons in the morning. There were 5,975 pink balloons at the factory at the end of the day. How many pink balloons did the factory workers make in the afternoon?

_____

_____

Show your work.

▶ Practice Solving Problems (continued)

19. Terrence is planning a 760-mile trip. He travels 323 miles the first two days. How many miles does Terrence have left to travel on this trip?

_____

_____

20. There were some people at the football stadium early last Sunday, and then 5,427 more people arrived. Then there were 79,852 people at the stadium. How many people arrived early?

_____

_____

▶ What's the Error?

Dear Math Students,

The problem shown below was part of my homework assignment.

Mrs. Nason has a collection of 1,845 stamps. She bought some more stamps. Now she has 2,270 stamps. How many stamps did Mrs. Nason buy?

To solve the problem, I wrote this equation: $s - 1,845 = 2,270$. I solved the equation and wrote $s = 4,115$.

My teacher says that my answer is not correct. Can you help me understand what I did wrong and explain how to find the correct answer?

Your Friend,
Puzzled Penguin

21. Write a response to Puzzled Penguin.

_____

Situation and Solution Equations for Addition and Subtraction

► Discuss Inverse Operations

Multiplication and division are inverse operations.
They undo each other.

A **factor pair** for a number is a pair of whole
numbers whose product is that number. For
example, a factor pair for 15 is 3 and 5. A rectangle
model is a diagram that shows a factor pair and the
product.

1. Which numbers in the rectangle model above are
   the factors? Where are the factors located?

   _____

2. Which number is the product? Where is the product
   located?

   _____

A rectangle model can you help you find all eight related
multiplication and division equations for two factors. You
can write these equations for the rectangle model above.

$$63 = 7 \times 9 \qquad\qquad 7 \times 9 = 63$$
$$63 = 9 \times 7 \qquad\qquad 9 \times 7 = 63$$
$$7 = 63 \div 9 \qquad\qquad 63 \div 9 = 7$$
$$9 = 63 \div 7 \qquad\qquad 63 \div 7 = 9$$

3. Write the eight related multiplication and division
   equations for the rectangle model below.

12
8	96

   _____   _____

   _____   _____

   _____   _____

   _____   _____

▶ Write Equations to Solve Problems

Read the problem and answer the questions.

	n
9	234

4. Brenda planted 234 trees on her farm. The farm has 9 rows of trees. How many trees are in each row?

   a. The number of trees on the farm is known.
     Write the number.

   b. The number of rows of trees is known.
     Write the number.

   c. The number of trees in each row is unknown.
     Use the letter *n* to represent the number of
     trees in each row. Write a situation equation
     to solve the problem.

   d. Write a solution equation.

   e. Solve your equation.

Write an equation to solve the problem. Draw a model if you need to.

Show your work.

5. Evan is starting a cycling program. He will ride 315 miles each month for the next 6 months. How many miles does he plan to ride in all?

6. Suki has 152 stickers to place in a sticker album. How many pages will Suki fill with stickers if each page in the album holds 8 stickers?

7. Al bought a wall pattern with 27 rows of 28 squares. How many squares are in the wall pattern?

► Discuss Comparison Problems

To prepare for a family gathering, Sara and Ryan made
soup. Sara made 2 quarts. Ryan made 6 quarts.

You can **compare** amounts, using multiplication and division.

Let r equal the number of quarts Ryan made.
Let s equal the number of quarts Sara made.

Ryan made 3 times as many quarts as Sara.

$$r = 3 \cdot s, \ r = 3s, \text{ or } s = r \div 3$$

Ryan (r) | 2 | 2 | 2 | 6

Sarah (s) | 2 | 2 | 2

Solve.

Natasha made 12 quarts of soup. Manuel made 3 quarts.

1. Draw **comparison bars** to show the amount of soup each
   person made.

2. _____ made 4 times as many quarts as _____.

3. Write a multiplication equation that compares the
   amounts. _____

4. Write a division equation that compares the amounts.

   _____

5. Multiplication is the putting together of equal groups.
   How can this idea be used to explain why a *times as
   many* comparing situation is multiplication?

   _____

   _____

▶ **Share Solutions**

Write an equation to solve each problem.
Draw a model if you need to.

Show your work.

6. There are 24 students in the science club. There are 2 times as many students in the drama club. How many students are in the drama club?

   a. Draw comparison bars to compare the numbers of students in each club.

   b. Write an equation to solve the problem.

   _____

7. There are 180 pennies in Miguel's coin collection and that is 5 times as many as the number of quarters in his coin collection. How many quarters does Miguel have?

   _____

8. Fred has 72 football cards and Scott has 6 football cards. How many times as many football cards does Fred have as Scott has?

   _____

9. Audrey has 1,263 centimeters of fabric, and that is 3 times as much fabric as she needs to make some curtains. How many centimeters of fabric does Audrey need to make the curtains?

   _____

Multiplication Comparisons

VOCABULARY
comparison situations

▶ **Discuss Comparison Situations**

In Lesson 4-4, you learned about multiplication and division **comparison situations**. You can also compare by using addition and subtraction. You can find *how much more* or *how much less* one amount is than another.

The amount more or less is called the difference. In some problems, the difference is not given. You have to find it. In other problems, the lesser or the greater amount is not given.

Mai has 9 apples and 12 plums.

- How many more plums than apples does Mai have?

- How many fewer apples than plums does Mai have?

Plums	12	
Apples	9	d

Comparison bars can help us show which is more. We show the difference in an oval.

Draw comparison bars for each problem. Write and solve an equation. Discuss other equations you could use.

1. A nursery has 70 rose bushes and 50 tea-tree bushes. How many fewer tea-tree bushes than rose bushes are at the nursery?

2. Dan wants to plant 30 trees. He has dug 21 holes. How many more holes does Dan need to dig?

▶ Share Solutions

Draw comparison bars for each problem.
Write and solve an equation.

Show your models here.

3. Kyle and Mackenzie are playing a computer game. Kyle scored 7,628 points. Mackenzie scored 2,085 fewer points than Kyle. How many points did Mackenzie score?

_____

4. The school fair fundraiser made $632 more from baked goods than from games. The school fair made $935 from games. How much money did the school fair make from baked goods?

_____

5. A college football stadium in Michigan seats 109,901 people. A college football stadium in Louisiana seats 92,542 people. How many fewer people does the stadium in Louisiana seat than the stadium in Michigan?

_____

6. The soccer team drilled for 150 minutes last week. The team drilled for 30 minutes more than it scrimmaged. For how long did the team scrimmage?

_____

Discuss Comparison Problems

▶ Solve Comparison Problems

Show your models here.

For each problem, draw a model and write *addition* or *multiplication* to identify the type of comparison. Then write and solve an equation to solve the problem.

7. Nick and Liz both collect marbles. Liz has 4 times as many marbles as Nick. If Nick has 240 marbles, how many marbles does Liz have?

   Type of comparison: _____

   Equation and answer: _____

8. Samantha has 145 fewer songs on her portable media player than Luke has on his portable media player. If Samantha has 583 songs, how many songs does Luke have?

   Type of comparison: _____

   Equation and answer: _____

9. A large bookstore sold 19,813 books on Saturday and 22,964 books on Sunday. How many fewer books did the bookstore sell on Saturday than on Sunday?

   Type of comparison: _____

   Equation and answer: _____

10. Last weekend, Mr. Morgan rode his bike 3 miles. This weekend, he rode his bike 21 miles. How many times as many miles did Mr. Morgan ride his bike this weekend as last weekend?

    Type of comparison: _____

    Equation and answer: _____

    _____

▶ Practice

Write and solve an equation to solve each problem.
Draw comparison bars when needed.

Show your work.

11. On the last day of school, 100 more students wore shorts than wore jeans. If 130 students wore jeans, how many students wore shorts?

_____

12. Matthew completed a puzzle with 90 pieces. Wendy completed a puzzle with 5 times as many pieces. How many pieces are in Wendy's puzzle?

_____

13. There were 19,748 adults at a baseball game. There were 5,136 fewer children at the baseball game than there were adults. How many children were at the baseball game?

_____

▶ What's the Error?

Dear Math Students,

I was asked to find the number of stamps that Amanda has if her friend Jesse has 81 stamps and that is 9 times as many stamps as Amanda has.

To solve the problem, I wrote this equation: 81 x 9 = *s*. I solved the equation and wrote *s* = 729. My teacher says that my answer is not correct. Can you help me understand what I did wrong?

Your friend,
Puzzled Penguin

14. Write a response to Puzzled Penguin.

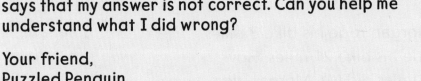

_____

_____

Discuss Comparison Problems

VOCABULARY
pictograph

▶ Use a Pictograph

A **pictograph** is a graph that uses pictures or symbols to represent data. This pictograph shows how many books 5 students checked out of a library in one year.

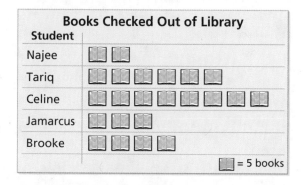

Use the pictograph to solve.

1. Write an addition equation and a subtraction equation that compare the number of books Tariq checked out (t) to the number of books Jamarcus checked out (j).

_____

2. Write a multiplication equation and a division equation that compare the number of books Najee checked out (n) to the number of books Celine checked out (c).

_____

3. Celine checked out twice as many books as which student?

_____

4. Which student checked out 30 fewer books than Celine?

_____

5. The number of books Dawson checked out is not shown. If Jamarcus checked out 10 more books than Dawson, how many books did Dawson check out?

_____

▶ Use a Bar Graph

The bar graph below shows the number of home runs hit by five members of a baseball team.

Use the bar graph to solve.

6. Write an addition equation and a subtraction equation that compare the number of home runs Suzy hit (*s*) to the number of home runs Kim hit (*k*).

   _____

7. Write a multiplication equation and a division equation that compare the number of home runs Greta hit (*g*) to the number of runs Fred hit (*f*).

   _____

8. How many more home runs did Von hit than Greta?

   _____

9. Which player hit 10 fewer home runs than Von?

   _____

10. This year, Fred hit 2 times as many home runs as he hit last year. How many home runs did Fred hit last year?

    _____

11. **Math Journal** Write a sentence about the graph that contains the words *times as many*.

Graphs and Comparison Problems

▶ Discuss the Steps of the Problem

Sometimes you will need to work through more than one step to solve a problem. The steps can be shown in one or more equations.

Solve.

1. At Parkes Elementary School, there are 6 fourth-grade classes with 17 students in each class. On Friday, 23 fourth-graders brought lunch from home and the rest of the students bought lunch in the cafeteria. How many fourth-graders bought lunch in the cafeteria on Friday?

   _____

2. Solve the problem again by finishing Tommy's and Lucy's methods. Then discuss how the two methods are alike and how they are different.

Tommy's Method	Lucy's Method
Write an equation for each step.	**Write an equation for the whole problem.**
Find the total number of students who are in fourth grade.	Let n = the number of students who bought lunch.
$6 \times 17 = $ _____	Students in each fourth grade class. Students who brought lunch from home.
Subtract the number of students who brought lunch from home.	$6 \quad \times \quad \underline{\hspace{1cm}} \quad - \quad \underline{\hspace{1cm}} \quad = n$
$102 - 23 = $ _____	$\underline{\hspace{1cm}} = n$

3. Use an equation to solve. Discuss the steps you used.

   Susan buys 16 packages of hot dogs for a barbecue. Each package contains 12 hot dogs. Hot-dog buns are sold in packages of 8. How many packages of hot-dog buns does Susan need to buy so she has one bun for each hot dog?

   _____

▶ Share Solutions

Use an equation to solve.   *Show your work.*

4. Admission to the theme park is $32 for each adult.
   A group of 5 adults and 1 child pays $182 to enter
   the theme park. How much is a child's ticket to the
   theme park?

   _____

5. Kenny collects CDs and DVDs. He has a total of 208 CDs.
   He also has 8 shelves with 24 DVDs on each shelf.
   How many more CDs does Kenny have than DVDs?

   _____

6. Carla plants 14 tomato plants. Her gardening book says
   that each plant should grow 12 tomatoes. She plans to
   divide the tomatoes equally among herself and 7 friends.
   How many tomatoes would each person get?

   _____

7. Alex and his family go on a roadtrip. On the first
   day, they drive 228 miles. On the second day, they
   drive 279 miles. Their destination is 1,043 miles away.
   How many miles do they have left to drive to reach
   their destination?

   _____

8. A public library has more than 50,000 books. There are
   249 science books and 321 technology books. Mary
   sorts the science and technology books on shelves
   with 6 books on each shelf. How many shelves will
   Mary fill with science and technology books?

   _____

▶ Discuss the Steps

1. Mr. Stills makes bags of school supplies for the 9 students in his class. He has 108 pencils and 72 erasers. He puts the same number of pencils and the same number of erasers into each bag. How many more pencils than erasers are in each bag of school supplies?

Solve the problem by finishing Nicole's and David's methods. Discuss what is alike and what is different about the methods.

Nicole's Method

Write an equation for each step.

Divide to find the number of pencils that Mr. Stills puts in each bag of school supplies. $\qquad$ $108 \div 9 = \underline{\hphantom{XXX}}$

Divide to find the number of erasers that Mr. Stills puts in each bag of school supplies. $\qquad$ $72 \div 9 = \underline{\hphantom{XXX}}$

Subtract the number of erasers in each bag from the number of pencils in each bag. $\qquad$ $12 - 8 = \underline{\hphantom{XXX}}$

There are $\underline{\hphantom{XXX}}$ more pencils than erasers in each bag of school supplies.

David's Method

Write an equation for the whole problem.

Let $p =$ how many more pencils than erasers are in each bag of school supplies

The number of pencils in each bag of school supplies.   The number of erasers in each bag of school supplies.

$$\underline{\hphantom{XXX}} \div 9 - \underline{\hphantom{XXX}} \div 9 = p$$
$$12 - 8 = p$$
$$\underline{\hphantom{XXX}} = p$$

There are $\underline{\hphantom{XXX}}$ more pencils than erasers in each bag of school supplies.

▶ Discuss the Steps (continued)

2. John is selling bags of popcorn for a school fundraiser. So far, John has sold 45 bags of popcorn for $5 each. His goal is to earn $300 for the school fundraiser. How many more bags of popcorn must John sell to reach his goal?

Solve the problem by writing an equation for each step. Then solve the problem by writing one equation for the whole problem.

Write an equation for each step.

Multiply to find how much money John has earned so far selling popcorn.

$$\underline{\hspace{2cm}} \times \quad \$5 \quad = \quad \$\underline{\hspace{1.5cm}}$$

Subtract to find how much money John has left to earn to reach his goal.

$$\$300 \quad - \quad \$\underline{\hspace{1.5cm}} \quad = \quad \$\underline{\hspace{1.5cm}}$$

Divide to find the number of bags of popcorn John must sell to reach his goal.

$$\$75 \quad \div \quad \$5 \quad = \quad \underline{\hspace{2cm}}$$

John must sell _____ more bags of popcorn to reach his goal.

Write an equation for the whole problem.

Let b = the number of bags of popcorn John must sell to reach his goal.

John's fundraiser   Amount of money John has
goal amount.   raised so far.

$$(\underline{\hspace{1.5cm}} - \underline{\hspace{1.5cm}} \times \quad \$5) \quad \div \quad \$5 \quad = b$$

$$(\$300 \quad - \$\underline{\hspace{1.5cm}}) \quad \div \quad \$5 \quad = b$$

$$\$\underline{\hspace{1.5cm}} \quad \div \quad \$5 \quad = b$$

$$\underline{\hspace{2cm}} \quad = b$$

John must sell _____ more bags of popcorn to reach his goal.

▶ Multistep Word Problems

Use an equation to solve.

Show your work.

3. Sara bought some bags of beads. Each bag had 9 beads and cost $2. Sara used the beads to make 18 necklaces, each with 25 beads. How much money did Sara pay for the beads for all of the necklaces that she made?

_____

4. There are 5 fourth-grade classes going on a field trip. Two of the classes have 16 students each and 3 of the classes have 17 students each. They are travelling in vans that hold 9 students each. How many vans must they have to transport all the students?

_____

5. A movie theater has 13 screens. On weekends, each screen shows a movie 7 times in one day. On weekdays, each screen shows a movie 5 times in one day. How many more showings are there on Saturdays than on Tuesdays?

_____

6. Justin goes to the store and buys 3 T-shirts for $14 each. He also buys 2 pairs of jeans for $23 each. He gives the cashier $100. How much change does Justin receive?

_____

7. Terrence has 24 model cars arranged in equal rows of 6 model cars. Natalie has 18 model cars arranged in equal rows of 3 model cars. How many rows of model cars in all do they have?

_____

▶ What's the Error?

Dear Math Students,

My friend and I are planning a hike. We will hike from point *A* to point *B*, which is a distance of 28 miles. Then we will hike from Point *B* to Point *C*, which is a distance of 34 miles. We will walk 7 miles each day for 8 days. We are trying to figure out how many miles we need to walk on the ninth day to reach Point *C*.

I wrote and solved this equation.

$28 + 34 - 7 \times 8 = t$

$62 - 7 \times 8 = t$

$55 \times 8 = t$

$440 = t$

This answer doesn't make sense. Did I do something wrong? What do you think?

Your friend,
Puzzled Penguin

8. Write a response to Puzzled Penguin.

_____

_____

_____

_____

_____

► **Discuss Multistep Word Problems**

Use equations to solve.

Show your work.

1. Eli reads 6 pages in a book each night. Shelby reads 8 pages each night. How many pages altogether will Eli and Shelby read in one week?

2. Min Soo is ordering 5 pizzas for a party. Each pizza will be cut into 8 slices. Three pizzas will have multiple toppings, and the others will be plain cheese. How many slices of plain cheese pizza is Min Soo ordering for the party?

3. Jasmine and Mori each received the same number of party favor bags at a friend's party. Each bag contained 8 favors. If Jasmine and Mori received a total of 48 favors, how many party favor bags did they each receive?

4. In art class, Ernesto made some fruit bowls for his mother and brother. Nine apples can be placed in each bowl. Ernesto's brother placed 18 apples in the bowls he was given, and Ernesto's mother placed 36 apples in the bowls she was given. How many fruit bowls did Ernesto make?

5. On Tuesday, a bicycle shop employee replaced all of the tires on 6 bicycles. On Wednesday, all of the tires on 5 tricycles were replaced. What is the total number of tires that were replaced on those days?

► Solve Multistep Word Problems

Use equations to solve.

Show your work.

6. Mrs. Luong bought 9 trees for $40 each. She paid
   for her purchase with four $100 bills. How much
   change did she receive?

   _____

7. Chan Hee is carrying a box that weighs 37 pounds.
   In the box are five containers of equal weight, and
   a book that weighs 2 pounds. What is the weight
   of each container?

   _____

8. A pet shop is home to 6 cats, 10 birds, 3 dogs,
   and 18 tropical fish. Altogether, how many legs
   do those pets have?

   _____

9. Dan has 7 fish in his aquarium. Marilyn has
   4 times as many fish in her aquarium. How many
   fish do Dan and Marilyn have altogether?

   _____

10. Write a problem that is solved using more than
    one step. Then show how to solve the problem.

    _____

    _____

    _____

    _____

    _____

    _____

▶ Find Factor Pairs

A factor pair for a number is two whole numbers whose product is that number. For example, 2 and 5 is a factor pair for 10.

1. Draw arrays to show all the factor pairs for 12 on the grid below. The array for 1 and 12 is shown.

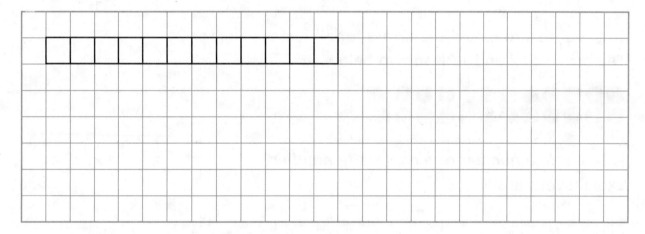

2. List all the factor pairs for 12. _____

Use the table to find all the factors pairs for each number.

3. 32

1	32
2	

4. 44

1	44

5. 100

1	100

List all the factor pairs for each number.

6. 29

7. 63

_____   _____

VOCABULARY
prime number
composite number

▶ Identify Prime and Composite Numbers

A number greater than 1 that has 1 and itself as its only factor pair is a **prime number**. Some prime numbers are 2, 5, 11, and 23.

A number greater than 1 that has more than one factor pair is a **composite number**. Some composite numbers are 4, 12, 25, and 100.

The number 1 is neither prime nor composite.

8. Use counters to model the arrays for all factor pairs for 24. The array for 2 and 12 is shown below.

9. Is 24 a *prime number* or a *composite number*? Explain your answer.

_____

_____

Write whether each number is *prime* or *composite*.

10. 99

11. 72

12. 31

_____

_____

_____

13. 45

14. 19

15. 88

_____

_____

_____

16. 67

17. 100

18. 53

_____

_____

_____

19. Is 2 the only even prime number? Explain.

_____

_____

▶ Factors and Multiples

A **multiple** of a number is a product of that number and a counting number.

20. What are the first five multiples of 4? Explain your method.

_____

_____

21. Write the first ten multiples of 8.

_____

22. Is 54 a multiple of 6? Explain how you know.

_____

_____

23. Is 6 a factor of 40? Explain how you know.

_____

24. What are the first five multiples of 9? Explain your method.

_____

_____

25. What are the factors of 63?

_____

26. Is 63 a multiple of each factor that you listed for Exercise 25? Explain how you know.

_____

_____

► Practice With Factors and Multiples

Tell whether 7 is a factor of each number. Write _yes_ or _no_.

27. 7   28. 84   29. 93   30. 49

_____   _____   _____   _____

Tell whether each number is a multiple of 9. Write _yes_ or _no_.

31. 27   32. 30   33. 81   34. 99

_____   _____   _____   _____

Use a pattern to find the unknown multiples.

35. $3 \times 11 = 33$ 36. $5 \times 6 = 30$

   $4 \times 11 = 44$ $6 \times 6 =$ _____

   $5 \times 11 =$ _____ $7 \times 6 =$ _____

   $6 \times 11 =$ _____ $8 \times 6 =$ _____

   $7 \times 11 =$ _____ $9 \times 6 =$ _____

Use the rule to complete the pattern.

37. Rule: skip count by 6

   6, _____, _____, 24, _____, 36, _____, 48, _____, 60

38. Rule: skip count by 5

   5, 10, _____, 20, 25, _____, 35, 40, _____, _____, 55, _____

39. Rule: skip count by 7

   7, 14, 21, _____, _____, _____, _____, _____, _____, _____

40. Rule: skip count by 12

   12, 24, _____, _____, _____, _____, _____, _____, _____

Factors and Prime Numbers

VOCABULARY
pattern

▶ Numerical Patterns

A **pattern** is a sequence that can be described by a rule.

Use the rule to find the next three terms in the pattern.

1. 22, 24, 26, 28, 30, …
Rule: add 2

_____

2. 5, 10, 20, 40, …
Rule: multiply by 2

_____

3. 1, 3, 9, 27, …
Rule: multiply by 3

_____

4. 2, 9, 16, 23, 30, …
Rule: add 7

_____

Use the rule to find the first ten terms in the pattern.

5. First term: 9   Rule: add 5

_____

6. First term: 10   Rule: add 60

_____

▶ Real World Applications

Solve.

7. Amy lives in the twentieth house on Elm Street. The first house on Elm Street is numbered 3. The second is 6. The third is 9. The fourth is 12. If this pattern continues, what is Amy's house number likely to be?

House	1st	2nd	3rd	4th	20th
Number	3	6	9	12	

_____

8. Theo runs 5 miles every morning. He tracks his progress on a chart to log how many miles he has run in all. How many miles will Theo write on the 100th day?

Day	1	2	3	4	5	100
Miles	5	10	15	20	25	

_____

► Extend Patterns

9. What are the repeating terms of the pattern?

_____

10. What will be the tenth term in the pattern? _____

11. What will be the fifteenth term in the pattern? _____

► Growing Patterns

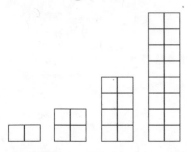

12. How does each figure in the pattern change from one term to the next?

_____

_____

13. Describe the number of squares in the next term in the pattern?

_____

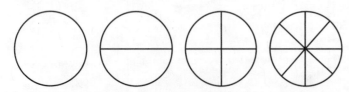

14. How does each figure in the pattern change from one term to the next?

_____

15. How many equal parts will be in the seventh term?

_____

Analyze Patterns

► Math and Pottery

Pottery are objects that are first shaped of wet clay and then hardened by baking. Four steps are needed to make a pottery product: preparing the clay mixture, shaping the clay, decorating and glazing the product, and baking the product. Pottery includes products such as works of art, dinnerware, vases, and other household items. Some of the places you can find pottery include art studios, crafts shows, pottery stores, and most households.

Write an equation to solve.

Show your work.

1. A small pottery store has 9 boxes full of pottery items. The boxes weigh 765 pounds in all. How much does each box weigh?

2. Julio and Myra had a pottery stand at the annual craft fair. They sold some of their pottery at the original price of $13 each and made $780. Later in the day, they decreased the price of each item by $4 and sold 20 more items. How much money did they make in all that day?

Write an equation to solve.

Show your work.

3. Last month, Mr. Smith bought 65 small cans of paint for his pottery shop. This month he bought 3 times as many small cans of paint. How many small cans of paint did he buy this month?

_____

4. The employees at a pottery warehouse are packing boxes of vases to be delivered by truck. They packed 824 small vases in boxes that each hold 8 vases. They also packed 296 large vases in boxes that each hold 4 vases. How many boxes did the workers pack in all?

_____

5. Last year, there were 3,875 different pottery items for sale at a large crafts show. This year, there were 1,260 fewer pottery items for sale at the crafts show. How many pottery items were for sale at the crafts show this year?

_____

Solve.

6. Isabella saw a pottery design that she liked at a crafts store. She wants to copy the design and paint it on a pot she is making. Part of the design is shown below.

a. What shape should Isabella paint next to continue the design's pattern?

_____

b. What will be the fourteenth term in Isabella's design?

_____

Focus on Mathematical Practices

VOCABULARY
composite number
prime number
situation equation
solution equation

▶ Vocabulary

Choose the best term from the box.

1. A _____ shows the operation that can be used to solve a problem. (Lessons 4-2, 4-3)

2. A number greater than 1 that has 1 and itself as its only factor pair is a _____ (Lesson 4-10)

3. A _____ shows the structure of the information in a problem. (Lessons 4-2, 4-3)

▶ Concepts and Skills

4. Explain how the equation for *4 is 2 more than 2* is different from the equation for *4 is 2 times as many as 2*.
(Lessons 4-4, 4-5, 4-6)

_____

_____

_____

5. Explain how you could use rectangles and circles to show the following pattern: A B B A B B A B B. (Lesson 4-11)

_____

_____

6. Dori wrote this problem: Mrs. Ramos has 1,352 stamps. She buys some more stamps. Now she has 1,943 stamps. How many stamps did she buy? Explain why the situation equation $1,352 + s = 1,943$ represents Dori's problem. (Lesson 4-2)

_____

_____

_____

Solve for ☐ **or** *n*. (Lesson 4-1)

7. $(18 - 9) \cdot 3 = $ ☐ $\cdot 3$

☐ = _____

8. $(35 + 50) - (25 \div 5) = n$

$n = $ _____

List all factor pairs for each number. (Lesson 4-10)

9. 47

_____

10. 28

_____

Write whether each number is *prime* **or** *composite*. (Lesson 4-10)

11. 98

_____

12. 61

_____

Tell whether each number is a multiple of 7. Write *yes* **or** *no*. (Lesson 4-10)

13. 36

_____

14. 84

_____

Use the rule to find the next three terms in the pattern. (Lesson 4-11)

15. 6, 12, 24, 48, …
Rule: multiply by 2

_____

16. 55, 95, 135, 175, …
Rule: add 40

_____

17. 4, 12, 36, 108, …
Rule: multiply by 3

_____

Describe the next term of each pattern. (Lesson 4-11)

18. ▲■□□▲■□□▲■□□▲

_____

19. (dot pattern figures)

_____

► Problem Solving

For Problems 20–21, write an equation to solve the problem.
(Lessons 4-2, 4-3)

20. The Appalachian Trail is a hiking trail that runs from Maine to Georgia and is approximately 2,160 miles long. Suppose the Andersons want to hike 9 miles per day along an 864-mile section of the trail from New York to Georgia. On how many days will the Andersons hike 9 miles?

_____

_____

21. The library had a large collection of books. Then the librarian ordered 2,200 more books. Now there are 13,327 books. How many books did the library have at the start?

_____

_____

For Problems 22–23, use the pictograph. Write an equation to solve each comparison problem. (Lessons 4-4, 4-5, 4-6)

Students' Field Trip Choices	
Zoo	☺ ☺ ☺
Science Center	☺ ☺ ☺ ☺ ☺ ☺
Aquarium	☺ ☺ ☺ ☺ ☺ ☺ ☺
Art Museum	☺ ☺

☺ = 4 votes

22. How many fewer students voted for the zoo than voted for the aquarium?

_____

23. How many times as many students voted for the science center as voted for the art museum?

_____

For Problems 24–25, use an equation to solve.
(Lessons 4-7, 4-8, 4-9)

24. Rita and Cody sold refreshments at the football game. They sold 6 sandwiches, 8 bags of popcorn, and 20 bottles of water. The sandwiches cost $5 each. The bags of popcorn cost $2 each. The bottles of water cost $1 each. How much money in all did Rita and Cody make?

_____

25. **Extended Response** A bakery had 2 trays with 28 muffins on each tray. The bakery had 4 trays of cupcakes with 12 cupcakes on each tray. On Monday, the bakery sold 12 cupcakes.

a. How many muffins and cupcakes were left in all? Explain.

_____

_____

_____

b. How can you determine if your answer is reasonable?

_____

_____

Reference Tables

Table of Measures

Metric	Customary
Length/Area	
1,000 millimeters (mm) = 1 meter (m)	1 foot (ft) = 12 inches (in.)
100 centimeters (cm) = 1 meter	1 yard (yd) = 36 inches
10 decimeters (dm) = 1 meter	1 yard = 3 feet
1 dekameter (dam) = 10 meters	1 mile (mi) = 5,280 feet
1 hectometer (hm) = 100 meters	1 mile = 1,760 yards
1 kilometer (km) = 1,000 meters	
Liquid Volume	
1,000 milliliters (mL) = 1 liter (L)	6 teaspoons (tsp) = 1 fluid ounce (fl oz)
100 centiliters (cL) = 1 liter	2 tablespoons (tbsp) = 1 fluid ounce
10 deciliters (dL) = 1 liter	1 cup (c) = 8 fluid ounces
1 dekaliter (daL) = 10 liters	1 pint (pt) = 2 cups
1 hectoliter (hL) = 100 liters	1 quart (qt) = 2 pints
1 kiloliter (kL) = 1,000 liters	1 gallon (gal) = 4 quarts
Mass	**Weight**
1,000 milligrams (mg) = 1 gram (g)	1 pound (lb) = 16 ounces
100 centigrams (cg) = 1 gram	1 ton (T) = 2,000 pounds
10 decigrams (dg) = 1 gram	
1 dekagram (dag) = 10 grams	
1 hectogram (hg) = 100 grams	
1 kilogram (kg) = 1,000 grams	
1 metric ton = 1,000 kilograms	

© Houghton Mifflin Harcourt Publishing Company

Table of Units of Time

Time

1 minute (min) = 60 seconds (sec)

1 hour (hr) = 60 minutes

1 day = 24 hours

1 week (wk) = 7 days

1 month, about 30 days

1 year (yr) = 12 months (mo)
 or about 52 weeks

1 year = 365 days

1 leap year = 366 days

1 decade = 10 years

1 century = 100 years

1 millennium = 1,000 years

Table of Formulas

Perimeter

Polygon

P = sum of the lengths of the sides

Rectangle

$P = 2(l + w)$ or $P = 2l + 2w$

Square

$P = 4s$

Area

Rectangle

$A = lw$ or $A = bh$

Square

$A = s \cdot s$

Properties of Operations

Associative Property of Addition
$(a + b) + c = a + (b + c)$ $(2 + 5) + 3 = 2 + (5 + 3)$

Commutative Property of Addition
$a + b = b + a$ $4 + 6 = 6 + 4$

Addition Identity Property of 0
$a + 0 = 0 + a = a$ $3 + 0 = 0 + 3 = 3$

Associative Property of Multiplication
$(a \cdot b) \cdot c = a \cdot (b \cdot c)$ $(3 \cdot 5) \cdot 7 = 3 \cdot (5 \cdot 7)$

Commutative Property of Multiplication
$a \cdot b = b \cdot a$ $6 \cdot 3 = 3 \cdot 6$

Multiplicative Identity Property of 1
$a \cdot 1 = 1 \cdot a = a$ $8 \cdot 1 = 1 \cdot 8 = 8$

Distributive Property of Multiplication over Addition
$a \cdot (b + c) = (a \cdot b) + (a \cdot c)$ $2 \cdot (4 + 3) = (2 \cdot 4) + (2 \cdot 3)$

Problem Types

Addition and Subtraction Problem Types

	Result Unknown	Change Unknown	Start Unknown
Add to	A glass contained $\frac{3}{4}$ cup of orange juice. Then $\frac{1}{4}$ cup of pineapple juice was added. How much juice is in the glass now? *Situation and solution equation:* [1] $\frac{3}{4} + \frac{1}{4} = c$	A glass contained $\frac{3}{4}$ cup of orange juice. Then some pineapple juice was added. Now the glass contains 1 cup of juice. How much pineapple juice was added? *Situation equation:* $\frac{3}{4} + c = 1$ *Solution equation:* $c = 1 - \frac{3}{4}$	A glass contained some orange juice. Then $\frac{1}{4}$ cup of pineapple juice was added. Now the glass contains 1 cup of juice. How much orange juice was in the glass to start? *Situation equation* $c + \frac{1}{4} = 1$ *Solution equation:* $c = 1 - \frac{1}{4}$
Take from	Micah had a ribbon $\frac{5}{6}$ yard long. He cut off a piece $\frac{1}{6}$ yard long. What is the length of the ribbon that is left? *Situation and solution equation:* $\frac{5}{6} - \frac{1}{6} = r$	Micah had a ribbon $\frac{5}{6}$ yard long. He cut off a piece. Now the ribbon is $\frac{4}{6}$ yard long. What is the length of the ribbon he cut off? *Situation equation:* $\frac{5}{6} - r = \frac{4}{6}$ *Solution equation:* $r = \frac{5}{6} - \frac{4}{6}$	Micah had a ribbon. He cut off a piece $\frac{1}{6}$ yard long. Now the ribbon is $\frac{4}{6}$ yard long. What was the length of the ribbon he started with? *Situation equation:* $r - \frac{1}{6} = \frac{4}{6}$ *Solution equation:* $r = \frac{4}{6} + \frac{1}{6}$

[1]A situation equation represents the structure (action) in the problem situation. A solution equation shows the operation used to find the answer.

	Total Unknown	Addend Unknown	Both Addends Unknown
Put Together/ Take Apart	A baker combines $1\frac{2}{3}$ cups of white flour and $\frac{2}{3}$ cup of wheat flour. How much flour is this altogether? *Math drawing:*[1] *Situation and solution equation:* $1\frac{2}{3} + \frac{2}{3} = f$	Of the $2\frac{1}{3}$ cups of flour a baker uses, $1\frac{2}{3}$ cups are white flour. The rest is wheat flour. How much wheat flour does the baker use? *Math drawing:* *Situation equation:* $2\frac{1}{3} = 1\frac{2}{3} + f$ *Solution equation:* $f = 2\frac{1}{3} - 1\frac{2}{3}$	A baker uses $2\frac{1}{3}$ cups of flour. Some is white flour and some is wheat flour. How much of each type of flour does the baker use? *Math drawing:* *Situation equation* $2\frac{1}{3} = f + w$

[1]These math drawings are called math mountains in Grades 1–3 and break apart drawings in Grades 4 and 5.

Problem Types continued

Addition and Subtraction Problem Types (continued)

	Difference Unknown	Greater Unknown	Smaller Unknown
Additive Comparison[1]	At a zoo, the female rhino weighs $1\frac{3}{5}$ tons. The male rhino weighs $2\frac{2}{5}$ tons. How much **more** does the **male rhino** weigh than the female rhino?	**Leading Language** At a zoo, the female rhino weighs $1\frac{3}{5}$ tons. The **male rhino** weighs $\frac{4}{5}$ **ton more** than the female rhino. How much does the male rhino weigh?	**Leading Language** At a zoo, the male rhino weighs $2\frac{2}{5}$ tons. The **female rhino** weighs $\frac{4}{5}$ **ton less** than the male rhino. How much does the female rhino weigh?
	At a zoo, the female rhino weighs $1\frac{3}{5}$ tons. The male rhino weighs $2\frac{2}{5}$ tons. How much **less** does the **female** rhino weigh than the male rhino?	**Misleading Language** At a zoo, the female rhino weighs $1\frac{3}{5}$ tons. The **female rhino** weighs $\frac{4}{5}$ **ton less** than the male rhino. How much does the male rhino weigh?	**Misleading Language** At a zoo, the male rhino weighs $2\frac{2}{5}$ tons. The **male rhino** weighs $\frac{4}{5}$ **ton more** than the female rhino. How much does the female rhino weigh?
	Math drawing:	*Math drawing:*	*Math drawing:*
	$2\frac{2}{5}$ / $1\frac{3}{5}$ $\;$ d	m / $1\frac{3}{5}$ $\;$ $\frac{4}{5}$	$2\frac{2}{5}$ / f $\;$ $\frac{4}{5}$
	Situation equation: $1\frac{3}{5} + d = 2\frac{2}{5}$ or $d = 2\frac{2}{5} - 1\frac{3}{5}$ *Solution equation:* $d = 2\frac{2}{5} - 1\frac{3}{5}$	*Situation and solution equation:* $1\frac{3}{5} + \frac{4}{5} = m$	*Situation equation* $f + \frac{4}{5} = 2\frac{2}{5}$ or $f = 2\frac{2}{5} - \frac{4}{5}$ *Solution equation:* $f = 2\frac{2}{5} - \frac{4}{5}$

[1]A comparison sentence can always be said in two ways. One way uses *more*, and the other uses *fewer* or *less*. Misleading language suggests the wrong operation. For example, it says *the female rhino weighs* $\frac{4}{5}$ *ton less than the male*, but you have to add $\frac{4}{5}$ ton to the female's weight to get the male's weight.

Multiplication and Division Problem Types

	Unknown Product	Group Size Unknown	Number of Groups Unknown
Equal Groups	A teacher bought 10 boxes of pencils. There are 20 pencils in each box. How many pencils did the teacher buy? *Situation and solution equation:* $p = 10 \cdot 20$	A teacher bought 10 boxes of pencils. She bought 200 pencils in all. How many pencils are in each box? *Situation equation:* $10 \cdot n = 200$ *Solution equation:* $n = 200 \div 10$	A teacher bought boxes of 20 pencils. She bought 200 pencils in all. How many boxes of pencils did she buy? *Situation equation* $b \cdot 20 = 200$ *Solution equation:* $b = 200 \div 20$

	Unknown Product	Unknown Factor	Unknown Factor
Arrays[1]	An auditorium has 60 rows with 30 seats in each row. How many seats are in the auditorium? *Math drawing:* 30 / 60 / s *Situation and solution equation:* $s = 60 \cdot 30$	An auditorium has 60 rows with the same number of seats in each row. There are 1,800 seats in all. How many seats are in each row? *Math drawing:* n / 60 / 1,800 *Situation equation:* $60 \cdot n = 1,800$ *Solution equation:* $n = 1,800 \div 60$	The 1,800 seats in an auditorium are arranged in rows of 30. How many rows of seats are there? *Math drawing:* 30 / r / 1,800 *Situation equation* $r \cdot 30 = 1,800$ *Solution equation:* $r = 1,800 \div 30$

[1]We use rectangle models for both array and area problems in Grades 4 and 5 because the numbers in the problems are too large to represent with arrays.

© Houghton Mifflin Harcourt Publishing Company

Multiplication and Division Problem Types (continued)

	Unknown Product	Unknown Factor	Unknown Factor
Area	Sophie's backyard is 80 feet long and 40 feet wide. What is the area of Sophie's backyard? *Math drawing:* 80 40 | A *Situation and solution equation:* $A = 80 \cdot 40$	Sophie's backyard has an area of 3,200 square feet. The length of the yard is 80 feet. What is the width of the yard? *Math drawing:* 80 w | 3,200 *Situation equation:* $80 \cdot w = 3,200$ *Solution equation:* $w = 3,200 \div 80$	Sophie's backyard has an area of 3,200 square feet. The width of the yard is 40 feet. What is the length of the yard? *Math drawing:* l 40 | 3,200 *Situation equation* $l \cdot 40 = 3,200$ *Solution equation:* $l = 3,200 \div 40$
Multiplicative Comparison	**Whole Number Multiplier** Sam has 4 times as many marbles as Brady has. Brady has 70 marbles. How many marbles does Sam have? *Math drawing:* s | 70 | 70 | 70 | 70 b | 70 *Situation and solution equation:* $s = 4 \cdot 70$	**Whole Number Multiplier** Sam has 4 times as many marbles as Brady has. Sam has 280 marbles. How many marbles does Brady have? *Math drawing:* *Situation equation:* $4 \cdot b = 280$ *Solution equation:* $b = 280 \div 4$	**Whole Number Multiplier** Sam has 280 marbles. Brady has 70 marbles. The number of marbles Sam has is how many times the number Brady has? *Math drawing:* *Situation equation* $m \cdot 70 = 280$ *Solution equation:* $m = 280 \div 70$

Vocabulary Activities

▶ Word Review PAIRS

Work with a partner. Choose a word from a current unit or a review word from a previous unit. Use the word to complete one of the activities listed on the right. Then ask your partner if they have any edits to your work or questions about what you described. Repeat, having your partner choose a word.

Activities

- ▶ Give the meaning in words or gestures.
- ▶ Use the word in the sentence.
- ▶ Give another word that is related to the word in some way and explain the relationship.

▶ Crossword Puzzle PAIRS OR INDIVIDUALS

Create a crossword puzzle similar to the example below. Use vocabulary words from the unit. You can add other related words, too. Challenge your partner to solve the puzzle.

Across

2. The answer to an addition problem

4. _____ and subtraction are inverse operations.

5. To put amounts together

6. When you trade 10 ones for 1 ten, you _____.

Down

1. The number to be divided in a division problem

2. The operation that you can use to find out how much more one number is than another.

3. A fraction with a numerator of 1 is a _____ fraction.

Vocabulary Activities (continued)

▶ Word Wall   PAIRS OR SMALL GROUPS

With your teacher's permission, start a word wall in your classroom. As you work through each lesson, put the math vocabulary words on index cards and place them on the word wall. You can work with a partner or a small group choosing a word and giving the definition.

▶ Word Web   INDIVIDUALS

Make a word web for a word or words you do not understand in a unit. Fill in the web with words or phrases that are related to the vocabulary word.

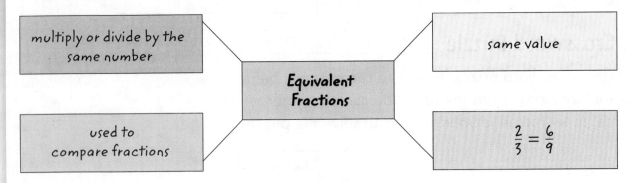

multiply or divide by the same number

same value

Equivalent Fractions

used to compare fractions

$\dfrac{2}{3} = \dfrac{6}{9}$

▶ Alphabet Challenge   PAIRS OR INDIVIDUALS

Take an alphabet challenge. Choose 3 letters from the alphabet. Think of three vocabulary words for each letter. Then write the definition or draw an example for each word.

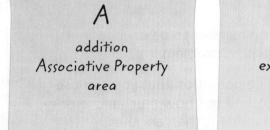

A

addition
Associative Property
area

E

equation
expanded form
estimate

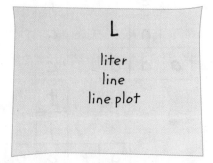

L

liter
line
line plot

▶ Concentration PAIRS

Write the vocabulary words and related words from a unit on index cards. Write the definitions on a different set of index cards. Mix up both sets of cards. Then place the cards facedown on a table in an array, for example, 3 by 3 or 3 by 4. Take turns turning over two cards. If one card is a word and one card is a definition that matches the word, take the pair. Continue until each word has been matched with its definition.

area

The number of square units that cover a figure.

▶ Math Journal INDIVIDUALS

As you learn new words, write them in your Math Journal. Write the definition of the word and include a sketch or an example. As you learn new information about the word, add notes to your definition.

Angle: A figure formed by two rays with the same endpoint.

Degree: A unit for measuring angles.

Vocabulary Activities (continued)

▶ What's the Word? PAIRS

Work together to make a poster or bulletin board display of
the words in a unit. Write definitions on a set of index cards.
Mix up the cards. Work with a partner, choosing a definition
from the index cards. Have your partner point to the word
on the poster and name the matching math vocabulary word.
Switch roles and try the activity again.

array

place value

addend

inverse operations

expanded form

word form

standard form

digit

one of two or more numbers added together to find a sum

Glossary

acute angle An angle smaller than a right angle.

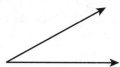

acute triangle A triangle with three acute angles.

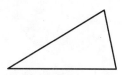

addend One of two or more numbers added together to find a sum.

Example: $7 + 8 = 15$

addend   addend   sum

adjacent (sides) Two sides that meet at a point.

Example: Sides *a* and *b* are adjacent.

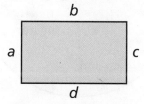

Algebraic Notation Method A strategy based on the Distributive Property in which a factor is decomposed to create simpler algebraic expressions, and the Distributive Property is applied.

Example: $9 \cdot 28 = 9 \cdot (20 + 8)$
$= (9 \cdot 20) + (9 \cdot 8)$
$= 180 + 72$
$= 252$

analog clock A clock with a face and hands.

angle A figure formed by two rays with the same endpoint.

area The number of square units that cover a figure.

array An arrangement of objects, symbols, or numbers in rows and columns.

Associative Property of Addition Grouping the addends in different ways does not change the sum.

Example: $3 + (5 + 7) = 15$
$(3 + 5) + 7 = 15$

Glossary (continued)

Associative Property of Multiplication
Grouping the factors in different ways does not change the product.

Example: $3 \times (5 \times 7) = 105$
$(3 \times 5) \times 7 = 105$

B

bar graph A graph that uses bars to show data. The bars may be vertical or horizontal.

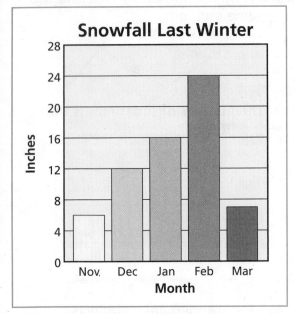

break-apart drawing A diagram that shows two addends and the sum.

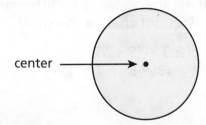

C

center The point that is the same distance from every point on the circle.

centimeter A unit of measure in the metric system that equals one hundredth of a meter. 100 cm = 1 m

circle A plane figure that forms a closed path so that all the points on the path are the same distance from a point called the center.

circle graph A graph that uses parts of a circle to show data.

Example:

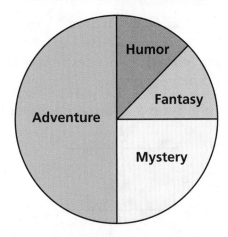

column A part of a table or array that contains items arranged vertically.

common denominator A common multiple of two or more denominators.

Example: A common denominator of $\frac{1}{2}$ and $\frac{1}{3}$ is 6 because 6 is a multiple of 2 and 3.

Commutative Property of Addition Changing the order of addends does not change the sum.

Example: $3 + 8 = 11$
$8 + 3 = 11$

Commutative Property of Multiplication Changing the order of factors does not change the product.

Example: $3 \times 8 = 24$
$8 \times 3 = 24$

compare Describe quantities as greater than, less than, or equal to each other.

comparison bars Bars that represent the larger amount and smaller amount in a comparison situation.

For addition and subtraction:

For multiplication and division:

smaller amount	smaller amount	smaller amount	larger amount
smaller amount			

comparison situation A situation in which two amounts are compared by addition or by multiplication. An *addition comparison situation* compares by asking or telling how much more (how much less) one amount is than another. A *multiplication comparison situation* compares by asking or telling how many times as many one amount is as another. The multiplication comparison may also be made using fraction language. For example, you can say, "Sally has one fourth as much as Tom has," instead of saying "Tom has 4 times as much as Sally has."

composite number A number greater than 1 that has more than one factor pair. Examples of composite numbers are 10 and 18. The factor pairs of 10 are 1 and 10, 2 and 5. The factor pairs of 18 are 1 and 18, 2 and 9, 3 and 6.

cup A unit of liquid volume in the customary system that equals 8 fluid ounces.

D

data A collection of information.

decimal number A representation of a number using the numerals 0 to 9, in which each digit has a value 10 times the digit to its right. A dot or **decimal point** separates the whole-number part of the number on the left from the fractional part on the right.

Examples: 1.23 and 0.3

Glossary (continued)

decimal point A symbol used to separate dollars and cents in money amounts or to separate ones and tenths in decimal numbers.

Examples:

decimal point

decimeter A unit of measure in the metric system that equals one tenth of a meter. 10 dm = 1 m

degree (°) A unit for measuring angles.

denominator The number below the bar in a fraction. It shows the total number of equal parts in the fraction.

Example:

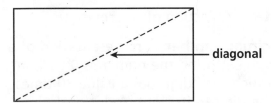

$\frac{3}{4}$ ← denominator

diagonal A line segment that connects vertices of a polygon, but is not a side of the polygon.

diagonal

difference The result of a subtraction.

Example: $54 - 37 = 17$ ← difference

digit Any of the symbols 0, 1, 2, 3, 4, 5, 6, 7, 8, or 9.

digital clock A clock that shows us the hour and minutes with numbers.

Digit-by-Digit A method used to solve a division problem.

Put in only one digit at a time.

$$
\begin{array}{r} 5 \\ 7\overline{)3{,}822} \\ -35 \\ \hline 32 \end{array}
\qquad
\begin{array}{r} 54 \\ 7\overline{)3{,}822} \\ -35 \\ \hline 32 \\ -28 \\ \hline 42 \end{array}
\qquad
\begin{array}{r} 546 \\ 7\overline{)3{,}822} \\ -35 \\ \hline 32 \\ -28 \\ \hline 42 \\ -42 \end{array}
$$

Distributive Property You can multiply a sum by a number, or multiply each addend by the number and add the products; the result is the same.

Example:
$$3 \times (2 + 4) = (3 \times 2) + (3 \times 4)$$

$$3 \times 6 \quad = \quad 6 \quad + \quad 12$$

$$18 \quad = \quad 18$$

dividend The number that is divided in division.

Example: $9\overline{)63}$ with quotient 7. 63 is the dividend.

divisible A number is divisible by another number if the quotient is a whole number with a remainder of 0.

divisor The number you divide by in division.

Example: $9\overline{)63}$ with quotient 7. 9 is the divisor.

dot array An arrangement of dots in rows and columns.

E

elapsed time The time that passes between the beginning and the end of an activity.

endpoint The point at either end of a line segment or the beginning point of a ray.

endpoint   endpoint   endpoint

equation A statement that two expressions are equal. It has an equal sign.

Examples: $32 + 35 = 67$
$67 = 32 + 34 + 1$
$(7 \times 8) + 1 = 57$

equilateral Having all sides of equal length.

Example: An equilateral triangle

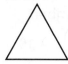

equivalent fractions Two or more fractions that represent the same number.

Example: $\frac{2}{4}$ and $\frac{4}{8}$ are equivalent because they both represent one half.

estimate A number close to an exact amount or to find about how many or how much.

evaluate Substitute a value for a letter (or symbol) and then simplify the expression.

expanded form A way of writing a number that shows the value of each of its digits.

Example: Expanded form of 835:
$800 + 30 + 5$
8 hundreds + 3 tens + 5 ones

Expanded Notation A method used to solve multiplication and division problems.

Examples:

43×67

$$
\begin{array}{r}
67 = 60 + 7 \\
\times\, 43 = 40 + 3 \\
\hline
40 \times 60 = 2400 \\
40 \times 7 \ = \ 280 \\
3 \times 60 \ = \ 180 \\
3 \times 7 \ = +\ 21 \\
\hline
2{,}881
\end{array}
$$

$3{,}822 \div 7$

$$
\begin{array}{r}
6 \\
40\ \rbrace 546 \\
500 \\
7\overline{)\,3{,}822} \\
-\ 3\ 500 \\
\hline
322 \\
-\ 280 \\
\hline
42 \\
-\ 42 \\
\hline
0
\end{array}
$$

expression One or more numbers, variables, or numbers and variables with one or more operations.

Examples: 4
$6x$
$6x - 5$
$7 + 4$

F

factor One of two or more numbers multiplied to find a product.

Example: $4 \times 5 = 20$

factor   factor   product

Glossary (continued)

factor pair A factor pair for a number is a pair of whole numbers whose product is that number.

Example: $5 \times 7 = 35$

factor pair   product

fluid ounce A unit of liquid volume in the customary system.
8 fluid ounces = 1 cup

foot A U.S. customary unit of length equal to 12 inches.

formula An equation with letters or symbols that describes a rule.

The formula for the area of a rectangle is:

$A = l \times w$

where A is the area, l is the length, and w is the width.

fraction A number that is the sum of unit fractions, each an equal part of a set or part of a whole.

Examples: $\frac{3}{4} = \frac{1}{4} + \frac{1}{4} + \frac{1}{4}$

$\frac{5}{4} = \frac{1}{4} + \frac{1}{4} + \frac{1}{4} + \frac{1}{4} + \frac{1}{4}$

G

gallon A unit of liquid volume in the customary system that equals 4 quarts.

gram The basic unit of mass in the metric system.

greater than (>) A symbol used to compare two numbers. The greater number is given first below.

Example: $33 > 17$
33 is greater than 17.

group To combine numbers to form new tens, hundreds, thousands, and so on.

H

hundredth A unit fraction representing one of one hundred parts, written as 0.01 or $\frac{1}{100}$.

7.634
↑
hundredth

one hundredth $= \frac{1}{100} = 0.01$

I

Identity Property of Multiplication The product of 1 and any number equals that number.

Example: $10 \times 1 = 10$

inch A U.S. customary unit of length.

Example: ⊢———————⊣
1 inch

inequality A statement that two expressions are not equal.

Examples: $2 < 5$
$4 + 5 > 12 - 8$

inverse operations Opposite or reverse operations that undo each other. Addition and subtraction are inverse operations. Multiplication and division are inverse operations.

Examples: $4 + 6 = 10$ so, $10 - 6 = 4$
and $10 - 4 = 6$.
$3 \times 9 = 27$ so, $27 \div 9 = 3$
and $27 \div 3 = 9$.

isosceles triangle A triangle with at least two sides of equal length.

K

kilogram A unit of mass in the metric system that equals one thousand grams. 1 kg = 1,000 g

kiloliter A unit of liquid volume in the metric system that equals one thousand liters. 1 kL = 1,000 L

kilometer A unit of length in the metric system that equals 1,000 meters. 1 km = 1,000 m

L

least common denominator The least common multiple of two or more denominators.

Example: The least common denominator of $\frac{1}{2}$ and $\frac{1}{3}$ is 6 because 6 is the smallest multiple of 2 and 3.

length The measure of a line segment or one side of a figure.

length

less than (<) A symbol used to compare two numbers. The smaller number is given first below.

Example: 54 < 78
54 is less than 78.

line A straight path that goes on forever in opposite directions.

Example: line *AB*

line of symmetry A line on which a figure can be folded so that the two halves match exactly.

line of symmetry

line plot A diagram that shows the frequency of data on a number line. Also called a dot plot.

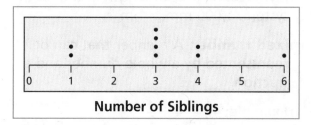

Number of Siblings

line segment Part of a line that has two endpoints.

line symmetry A figure has line symmetry if it can be folded along a line to create two halves that match exactly.

liquid volume A measure of the space a liquid occupies.

liter The basic unit of liquid volume in the metric system.
1 liter = 1,000 milliliters

Glossary (continued)

M

mass The measure of the amount of matter in an object.

meter The basic unit of length in the metric system.

metric system A base ten system of measurement.

mile A U.S. customary unit of length equal to 5,280 feet.

milligram A unit of mass in the metric system. 1,000 mg = 1g

milliliter A unit of liquid volume in the metric system. 1,000 mL = 1 L

millimeter A unit of length in the metric system. 1,000 mm = 1 m

mixed number A number that can be represented by a whole number and a fraction.

Example: $4\frac{1}{2} = 4 + \frac{1}{2}$

multiple A number that is the product of a given number and any whole number.

Examples:

$4 \times 1 = 4$, so 4 is a multiple of 4.
$4 \times 2 = 8$, so 8 is a multiple of 4.

N

number line A line that extends, without end, in each direction and shows numbers as a series of points. The location of each number is shown by its distance from 0.

numerator The number above the bar in a fraction. It shows the number of equal parts.

Example:

$$\frac{3}{4} \longleftarrow \text{numerator} \qquad \frac{3}{4} = \frac{1}{4} + \frac{1}{4} + \frac{1}{4}$$

O

obtuse angle An angle greater than a right angle and less than a straight angle.

obtuse triangle A triangle with one obtuse angle.

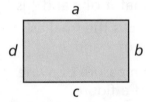

opposite sides Sides that are across from each other; they do not meet at a point.

Example: Sides a and c are opposite.

$$\begin{array}{c} a \\ d \; \boxed{} \; b \\ c \end{array}$$

Order of Operations A set of rules that state the order in which operations should be done.

STEPS: -Compute inside parentheses first.

-Multiply and divide from left to right.

-Add and subtract from left to right.

ounce A unit of weight.
16 ounces = 1 pound
A unit of liquid volume (also called a fluid ounce).
8 ounces = 1 cup

P

parallel Lines in the same plane that never intersect are parallel. Line segments and rays that are part of parallel lines are also parallel.

parallelogram A quadrilateral with both pairs of opposite sides parallel.

partial product The product of the ones, or tens, or hundreds, and so on in multidigit multiplication.

Example:

```
    24
 ×   9
    36   ←  partial product (9 × 4)
   180   ←  partial product (9 × 20)
   216
```

perimeter The distance around a figure.

perpendicular Lines, line segments, or rays are perpendicular if they form right angles.

Example: These two lines are perpendicular.

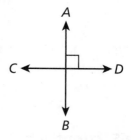

pictograph A graph that uses pictures or symbols to represent data.

Books Checked Out of Library	
Student	
Najee	📖 📖
Tariq	📖 📖 📖 📖 📖 📖
Celine	📖 📖 📖 📖 📖 📖 📖 📖
Jamarcus	📖 📖 📖
Brooke	📖 📖 📖 📖
	📖 = 5 books

pint A customary unit of liquid volume that equals 16 fluid ounces.

place value The value assigned to the place that a digit occupies in a number.

Example: 235

The 2 is in the hundreds place, so its value is 200.

Glossary (continued)

place value drawing A drawing that represents a number. Thousands are represented by vertical rectangles, hundreds are represented by squares, tens are represented by vertical lines, and ones by small circles.

Example:

2,697

Place Value Sections A method using rectangle drawings to solve multiplication or division problems.

point A location in a plane. It is usually shown by a dot.

polygon A closed plane figure with sides made of straight line segments.

pound A unit of weight in the U.S. customary system.

prefix A letter or group of letters placed before a word to make a new word.

prime number A number greater than 1 that has 1 and itself as the only factor pair. Examples of prime numbers are 2, 7, and 13. The only factor pair of 7 is 1 and 7.

product The answer to a multiplication problem.

Example: 9 × 7 = 63
↑
product

protractor A semicircular tool for measuring and constructing angles.

quadrilateral A polygon with four sides.

quart A customary unit of liquid volume that equals 32 ounces or 4 cups.

quotient The answer to a division problem.

Example: 7 is the quotient.

ray Part of a line that has one endpoint and extends without end in one direction.

rectangle A parallelogram with four right angles.

reflex angle An angle with a measure that is greater than 180° and less than 360°.

remainder The number left over after dividing two numbers that are not evenly divisible.

Example: $5)\overline{43}$ with 8 R3 The remainder is 3.

rhombus A parallelogram with sides of equal length.

right angle One of four angles made by perpendicular line segments.

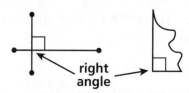

right angle

right triangle A triangle with one right angle.

round To find the nearest ten, hundred, thousand, or some other place value. The usual rounding rule is to round up if the next digit to the right is 5 or more and round down if the next digit to the right is less than 5.

Examples: 463 rounded to the nearest ten is 460.
463 rounded to the nearest hundred is 500.

row A part of a table or array that contains items arranged horizontally.

S

scalene A triangle with no equal sides is a scalene triangle.

Shortcut Method A strategy for multiplying. It is the current common method in the United States.

Step 1	Step 2
$\overset{7}{2}8$	$\overset{7}{2}8$
$\times\ 9$	$\times\ 9$
2	252

simplest form A fraction is in simplest form if there is no whole number (other than 1) that divides evenly into the numerator and denominator.

Example: $\frac{3}{4}$ This fraction is in simplest form because no number divides evenly into 3 and 4.

simplify an expression Combine like terms and perform operations until all terms have been combined.

simplify a fraction To divide the numerator and the denominator of a fraction by the same number to make an equivalent fraction made from fewer but larger unit fractions.

Example: $\frac{5}{10} = \frac{5 \div 5}{10 \div 5} = \frac{1}{2}$

situation equation An equation that shows the structure of the information in a problem.

Example: $35 + n = 40$

solution equation An equation that shows the operation that can be used to solve the problem.

Example: $n = 40 - 35$

square A rectangle with 4 sides of equal length and 4 right angles. It is also a rhombus.

square array An array in which the number of rows equals the number of columns.

square centimeter A unit of area equal to the area of a square with one-centimeter sides.

square decimeter A unit of area equal to the area of a square with one-decimeter sides.

square foot A unit of area equal to the area of a square with one-foot sides.

square inch A unit of area equal to the area of a square with one-inch sides.

square kilometer A unit of area equal to the area of a square with one-kilometer sides.

square meter A unit of area equal to the area of a square with one-meter sides.

square mile A unit of area equal to the area of a square with one-mile sides.

square millimeter A unit of area equal to the area of a square with one-millimeter sides.

square unit A unit of area equal to the area of a square with one-unit sides.

square yard A unit of area equal to the area of a square with one-yard sides.

standard form The form of a number written using digits.

Example: 2,145

straight angle An angle that measures 180°.

sum The answer when adding two or more addends.

Example:

$$53 + 26 = 79$$

addend   addend   sum

T

table Data arranged in rows and columns.

tenth A unit fraction representing one of ten equal parts of a whole, written as 0.1 or $\frac{1}{10}$.

12.34
↑
tenth

one tenth = $\frac{1}{10}$ = 0.1

term in an expression A number, variable, product, or quotient in an expression. Each term is separated by an operation sign (+, −).

Example: $3n + 5$ has two terms, $3n$ and 5.

thousandth A unit fraction representing one of one thousand equal parts of a whole, written as 0.001 or $\frac{1}{1,000}$.

ton A unit of weight that equals 2,000 pounds.

tonne A metric unit of mass that equals 1,000 kilograms.

total Sum. The result of addition.

Example: 53 + 26 = 79

addend   addend   total (sum)

trapezoid A quadrilateral with exactly one pair of parallel sides.

triangle A polygon with three sides.

© Houghton Mifflin Harcourt Publishing Company

---

unit A standard of measurement.

Examples: Centimeters, pounds, inches, and so on.

unit fraction A fraction whose numerator is 1. It shows one equal part of a whole.

Example: $\frac{1}{4}$

V

variable A letter or a symbol that represents a number in an algebraic expression.

vertex A point that is shared by two sides of an angle or two sides of a polygon.

vertex   vertex

W

width The measure of one side of a figure.

width

word form The form of a number written using words instead of digits.

Example: Six hundred thirty-nine

Y

yard A U.S. customary unit of length equal to 3 feet.